Poland Between East and West

Poland Between East and West

The Controversies over Self-Definition
and Modernization in Partitioned Poland

Andrzej Walicki

The August Zaleski Lectures
Harvard University, 18–22 April 1994

ISBN-10: 0-916458-71-7
ISBN-13: 978-0-916458-71-3

Distributed by Harvard University Press for the Ukrainian Research
Institute, Cambridge, Massachusetts, USA.

The Harvard Ukrainian Research Institute was established in 1973 as an
integral part of Harvard University. It supports research associates and
visiting scholars who are engaged in projects concerned with all aspects
of Ukrainian studies. The Institute also works in close cooperation with
the Committee on Ukrainian Studies, which supervises and coordinates
the teaching of Ukrainian history, language, and literature at Harvard
University.

Contents

Editorial Statement

The Ukrainian Research Institute at Harvard University has established the series Harvard Papers in Ukrainian Studies as a medium for occasional papers, reports, reprints, and long articles. The series is dedicated to a broad vision of Ukrainian studies. It thus will include works that have Ukraine alone as their central focus, others that deal with Ukraine in relation to its neighbors, and still others that focus mainly on Ukraine's neighbors, inasmuch as that focus ultimately is relevant to an understanding of Ukrainian history, culture, language, or politics. This last aspect of the series is meant to foster an understanding of Ukraine's place within the different spheres of its existence: as part of East Central Europe, as part of the Black Sea littoral, as part of the Polish-Lithuanian Commonwealth, as part of the Russian Empire. By understanding these different but interrelated spheres of Ukrainian existence, both past and present, it is hoped that a fuller understanding of an independent Ukraine will arise, both for specialists in Ukrainian studies and in other areas.

Poland Between East and West

The Commonwealth at its Farthest Extent, ca. 1620

From Sarmatianism to Romanticism

The Legacy of Sarmatianism and the Westernizing Reforms of the Enlightenment

It is often assumed that the Poles, unlike the Russians, have always seen themselves as belonging only to the West, and that they therefore could not perceive Western civilization as something alien to them that would threaten their traditional values. In contemporary Poland such claims are combined, as a rule, with a stress on an organic relationship between "Polishness" and Roman Catholicism, thus seeing Poland as a bastion of "Latin civilization." An alternative way of emphasizing Poland's organic and intransigent Westernism consists of taking up and applying to Poland Milan Kundera's concept of "Central Europe."[1] In both cases there is a clear statement of intent: Polish intellectuals use them as additional arguments for the goal of stimulating the quick inclusion of Poland into the European Community.

Historically, however, things were much less clear. The traditional concept of Poland as a "bulwark of Christianity" (*antemurale Christianitatis*) was not identical with the view of Poland as part and parcel of the West. On the contrary: it was a part of the "Sarmatian" ideology of the Polish-Lithuanian Commonwealth, a unifying myth of its multiethnic gentry. The main function of this myth was to stress the cultural uniqueness of "Sarmatia," its fundamental difference from everything Western, and the need to defend its institutions and customs against dangerous influences from the West. Paradoxically, the Sarmatians were much more tolerant of oriental influences which reached them through the Muslim peoples—Turks and Tartars—against whom the Sarmatian Commonwealth waged constant wars under the banner of the defense of Christianity. It is deeply symbolic that King Jan Sobieski, who defeated the Turks in the battle of Vienna (1683), and who thereby earned the title of the "Savior of Europe," was greatly interested in the fashions among Crimean Tartars, while remaining indifferent to the fashions in Paris (although he had a beloved French wife).[2] This peculiar "easternization" of Poland was a result of the transformation of the medieval, ethnically homogeneous Polish monarchy into a part of a multiethnic, multireligious, federal republic of the gentry, known as the Polish-Lithuanian Commonwealth. Let me briefly characterize this important change.

First and foremost, it was a shift from ethno-linguistic national patriotism to a form of multiethnic civic nationalism, based upon a vision of common political destiny and cemented by a fierce attachment to republican libertarian values. The nation of the gentry was conceived as a political, not an ethnic community, and it was precisely this that made it powerfully attractive to the gentry of the entire commonwealth, irrespective of their ethnicity and language. An influential sixteenth-century writer, Stanisław Orzechowski, was not mistaken in attributing this integrating effect to the attractiveness of Polish liberties.[3] Significantly, he was not a native Pole but a Polonized Ukrainian, who described himself as "gente Ruthenus, Natione Polonus"—politically a Pole, although ethnically a Ruthenian. This non-Polish ethnic background did not prevent him from seeing the Poles as a chosen nation and himself as a part of their mission.

Welding together different ethnic elements into a single cohesive nation involved a conscious creation of a national ideology. An important part of this ideology was purely political. Numerous writers promoted a new type of national pride, stemming from the image of the Jagellonian Commonwealth as a unique land of freedom. As ardent pupils of the ancients, they defined nation as a sovereign political community, using such terms as "*societas, civitas,* and *res publica.*" This was common not only in the sixteenth century, the period of Humanism and the "Golden Age" of the gentry democracy, but also in the seventeenth century—the time of Counter-Reformation and of the relative decline of the Commonwealth. Thus, for instance, a seventeenth-century writer and politician, Łukasz Opaliński, put forward a modern-sounding—and Western-sounding—theory about civil society (*societas civilis*), which arises from the development of human needs, and *republica* or *civitas*, as the large, organized society of an entire people (*magna illa unius populi civitas*), whose soul is the law.[4]

However, the ideologists of the "noble nation" were not satisfied with an exclusively political basis for national unity; they wanted to facilitate the process of integration by endowing the multiethnic nation with a feeling of being united by the common ancestry. This was done by claiming that the entire gentry of the Commonwealth constituted a "Sarmatian nation," descendants of the ancient, powerful, and famous Sarmatians. As a rule, this theory tended to identify the medieval history of the invented "Sarmatian nation" with Polish historical tradition; nevertheless, some writers made considerable efforts to integrate Polish history with the history of Kievan Rus' and Lithuania. Thus, for instance, Maciej Stryjkowski published a rich and interesting *Chronicle of Poland, Lithuania, Samogitia, and all Rus'* (*Kronika polska, litewska, żmudzka i wszystkiej Rusi;* 1582)—the first integrated history of all lands of the Commonwealth.[5] In the next century Wojciech Dębołęcki tried to integrate the history of Polish and Lithuanian-

Ruthenian nobility in a fantastic story of their common decent from the "Royal Sarmatians," descendants of the Scythians, whose history, in turn, derived directly from the Biblical Adam. He concluded from this that "Sarmatians" were the chosen nation, destined to rule over the world.[6]

It should be stressed that the multiethnic character of the "noble nation" must not be confused with a genuine multiculturalism. Membership in the gentry was open to different ethnic elements but offered little room for cultural autonomy. In the Lithuanian part of the Commonwealth baptized Jews were almost automatically ennobled, but this entailed a total cultural transformation: the new noble, *origine Judaeus,* had to dress himself as a Sarmatian, to grow a moustache, to carry a sabre, to ride a horse, and so forth.[7] This was so because the ideologists of Sarmatianism took it for granted that national culture should be homogeneous, and that the basis for cultural unification should be provided by the Polish culture, perceived as the most developed culture of the realm. At the same time, however, the expansion to the East and the Eastern-oriented politics of the Commonwealth weakened the Western character of Polish national consciousness. True, this did not happen at once. During the entire sixteenth century the Polish part of the Commonwealth was a flourishing European country. And yet, in the next century the effective integration of the Polish elite with the recently Polonized elites of Lithuania and Ukraine brought into being a new "Sarmatian" culture, an original synthesis of East and West, proud of its uniqueness and consciously turning away from Western royalism and moral corruption.

Political ideology of the "Sarmatian" gentry rested on three tenets: the idea of a "granary of Europe," the idea of the "bulwark of Christianity," and, most importantly, the view of the gentry republic as the perfect political system, one infinitely superior to Western monarchies. The first idea defined Poland as a country which was and would remain agrarian, due to both its own character and to the needs of its neighbors; the implication here was that Poland could avoid economic modernization on the Western model (on condition that its purchases of foreign industrial products not include luxury items, which were seen as corrupting the simplicity of rural life). The second idea served as the source of a deceptive feeling of security: the increasingly strong Western monarchies, it was argued, presented no threat to the Polish-Lithuanian Commonwealth because they understood that this Commonwealth was defending them against the onslaughts of the infidels. The third view claimed that the political system of the Commonwealth was perfect from the viewpoint of freedom, hence worthy of preservation at all costs. Since royal power, the potential enemy of freedom, was perceived as capable of mobilizing for its cause the majority of the members of the Diet (*Sejm*) it was necessary to find a reliable safeguard against undesirable innovation. As is well known, this device was found in the old principle of unanimity, or, to put it differently, in the notorious *liberum veto*, by which any single member of the gentry could veto the work of the entire Diet.

Based on these tenets the Sarmatian Commonwealth developed into a country greatly different from the rest of Europe. It was fully aware of this difference and proud of it; accordingly, it treated other countries, despite their increasing strength and prosperity, with self-righteous condescension, if not outright contempt. The result was that Russia, after the reforms of Peter I, looked more European in Western eyes than Poland did—despite the fact that the Polish gentry were ardent Catholics and could, as a rule, communicate in Latin.[8] On the other hand, the necessity of economic modernization, of increasing the country's military capacity and, above all, of strengthening the executive power by abandoning the excesses of the "golden freedom," was more and more evident. As a consequence, Polish patriotic reformers of the Age of Enlightenment embraced a program of drawing Poland closer to Europe—a program of the Europeanization of Sarmatia. Stanisław August, the last king of an independent Poland, tried initially to achieve this objective with the help of a Westernized Russia. Journalists of *Monitor*, a periodical close to the king, went so far as to praise Peter I as the "heroic" and "immortal" Westernizer of Russia.[9]

The parallel between Poland and Russia as representing two countries which equally needed "Europeanization" leads to a broader comparative perspective. Stanisław Staszic, one of the greatest thinkers of the Polish Enlightenment, was impressed by the similarities between the Sarmatian Commonwealth and Asian countries, mainly Turkey, and proclaimed the need for overcoming the "Asiatization" of Poland. Similar views were developed by certain nineteenth-century Polish thinkers, for instance, the ambitious and prolific philosopher Bronisław Trentowski (1808–1869), as well as by some professional historians.

The main concern of the Polish Enlighteners—their radical wing, headed by Hugo Kołłątaj—was to transform the Sarmatian "nation of the gentry" into a modern "nation of property owners," in which active citizenship (that is, political rights) would depend not on noble status but on property qualifications.[10] In visualizing this nation they consciously embraced the French concept of a culturally homogeneous nation, speaking the same language and living under the same laws. This view of nationhood, later called the "Jacobin conception of the nation," was deeply suspicious of regional and cultural differences, regarding them as incompatible with national unity and social modernization. In the Polish context this meant the unification of the law, the liquidation of the autonomous status of Lithuania, and programmatic Polonization of the entire population. The rights of religious minorities were to be respected, but only in strictly religious matters. Thus, for instance, Jews were to be deprived of their autonomous political and juridical institutions, subjected to Polish jurisdiction, forced to attend Polish schools, and to dress like other Poles; even their beards were to be cut off, as the beards of the boyars in Russia had been. The Commission for National Education—Kołłątaj's creation, which deserves to be recognized as the first ministry of education in Europe—was to serve as a powerful instrument for implementing this program of nationbuilding on the Western model. If Ernest Gellner is correct (and I think he is) in defining modern nationalism as a species or patriotism which favors cohesiveness and cultural homogeneity,[11] then Polish reformers of the Age of Enlightenment could be called the first modern nationalists in Poland.

In practice this new conception of nationhood entailed political centralization, hence a curtailment of the gentry's "republican freedom." The reformers wanted to avoid going too far in this direction. The revolutions in America and in France supported their conviction that the age of monarchies was passing away, and that Poland had a legitimate cause in defending its republican institutions. Kołłątaj even tried to argue that a reformed Poland would not be a real monarchy, but, rather "a republic with a king," since sovereignty would rest with the entire body of citizens. Nevertheless, executive power was to be strengthened and centralized, with the scope of its activity greatly broadened. The government of Poland (no longer Poland-Lithuania, but a nationally unified Poland) was to be an active organizer of national efforts, responsible not only for national defense and domestic law-enforcement, but also for national education and economic growth. Characteristically, the Polish reformers often endorsed the physiocratic concept of national wealth, but did so without embracing the "laissez-faire" part of the physiocratic doctrine. On the contrary: they thought about the economy in terms of a conscious economic policy which stimulated economic growth, and took it for granted that the government should actively intervene in the economic sphere, using techniques recommended by mercantilism, cameralism, and protectionism.

The defenders of Sarmatian freedom did not remain silent. They quickly learned how to "modernize" their republicanism by borrowing arguments from the liberal or republican Western theorists, such as Locke, Rousseau, and Mably. Even the republicanism of Michał Wielhorski, the main ideologist of the conservative Confederation of Bar (1768–1772), could not be reduced to a defence of feudal liberties—it was modern and "enlightened" enough to inspire Rousseau's *Considerations on the Government of Poland*, a treatise warmly sympathizing with the "gentry republic."[12] And at the time of the Great Diet (1788–1792) the modernizing element of the republican ideology was often coming to the fore as an alterative national program. This in turn paved the way for a "new republicanism," free from exclusive association with the nobility, advocating the extension of civil an political rights to all inhabitants of the state. An interesting representative of this current was Wojciech Turski (Adalbert, the Sarmatian), who took the side of the conservative magnates in opposing the "monarchical reform" in Poland while enthusiastically embracing the ideals of the French Revolution at the same time.[13]

The crowning achievement of the Westernizing reforms of the Great Diet was the famous May 3rd Constitution of 1791. This constitution abolished the much-abused forms of "ancient freedom" (*liberum veto*, free elections, confederations, and so on), and transformed the Polish-Lithuanian Commonwealth into a hereditary constitutional monarchy of a unified Polish nation, with a modern government (whose ministers were called "Guardians of the Law"), and biennial parliaments. Political rights were made dependent on the ownership of land, which meant that many burghers (owners of houses) were raised to the status of "active citizens," while the landless gentry, the notorious clients of the magnates, were deprived of political influence. Thus, not only were republican principles replaced by monarchical ones, but even the most cherished idea of the gentry democracy—the equality of all the nobles—was abandoned. Civic liberties, including religious liberty, were strongly safeguarded, though restricted to the nobles and burghers. Peasants received only the protection of the law, plus a vague promise of future emancipation through a series of voluntary agreements. Nevertheless, it was an undeniably progressive legislative work, laying the foundations for further progressive developments. Karl Marx, otherwise so severe in his judgments of the ruling classes, wrote about it as follows: "Despite its shortcomings, this constitution looms up against the background of Russo-Prusso-Austrian barbarism as the only work of liberty (*das einzige Freiheitswerk*) which Eastern Europe has ever created independently. And it emerged exclusively from the privileged class, from the nobility. The history of the world has never seen another example of such nobility of the nobility (*Adel des Adels*)."[14]

The constitution had no chance to become the supreme law of the country. It remained a piece of paper, greatly celebrated today as a *sui generis* "last will" of the independent Polish state. But it is almost forgotten that it had been revoked, in fact, by Tadeusz Kościuszko, the democratic leader of the national uprising of 1794, who declared that the form of political system in Poland would be determined by a new Diet. And it is rarely remembered that the legacy of the May 3rd Constitution was not accepted by the Polish democrats of the Romantic Epoch; that all of them— from moderates, like Joachim Lelewel, to extreme radicals, like Edward Dembowski—unequivocally rejected it as monarchical and sanctifying inequality and betraying Polish national values.

What were the reasons of these severe judgments? They were quite plain, not difficult to understand. As a program of national revival the May 3rd Constitution was indeed a rather conspicuous failure of imagination. It did very little to improve the situation of the peasants, certainly not enough to make them patriotically loyal to the existing Polish state. At the same time it disenfranchised the masses of the poor gentry, who might have been the clients of reactionary magnates but, nonetheless, could not be replaced as bearers of national consciousness and its disseminators among the non-noble population. It was not realistic to believe that a nation of the gentry could be transformed at one stroke into a nation of property owners. After the partitions, the petty gentry—despite all its shortcoming—became the main social basis of Polish movements for national independence. As a very populous stratum, having little to lose and endowed with a vivid sense of is civic and national rights, it proved to be an asset rather than a liability for Poland.

It seems justified to claim that the true "testament" of eighteenth-century Poland is to be found in the proclamations of the Kościuszko Uprising, not in the legislative acts of the great Diet. Kościuszko's main idea, taken up by the nineteenth-century Polish radicals, was to emancipate the peasants and thus make them Polish patriots. In his emigré pamphlet *Can the Poles Win Through to Independence? (Czy Polacy mogą się wybić na niepodległość?*; 1800)[15] he visualized the peasant masses, with scythes in their hands, fighting bravely for Poland and making it invincible. He believed this to be possible because the emancipated peasants would make Poland "the sixteen-million strong nation," galvanized to battle by the spirit of liberty. Reference to sixteen millions makes it clear that he saw as potential Poles all inhabitants of the former Commonwealth, irrespective of their language and religious affiliation.

The Controversy over the West in the Romantic Epoch

The period of Napoleonic wars, which followed the third partition of Poland, ended with the creation of the Kingdom of Poland—united with the Empire of Russia, but with its own liberal constitution, parliament (*Sejm*), and army. Although it occupied only a very small part of the pre-partitioned Polish territory (smaller, in fact, than the Napoleonic Duchy of Warsaw), it was, nonetheless, a separate kingdom, bearing the name of Poland, and capable of national development. It owed its existence to the pro-Russian Polish party, headed by Prince Adam Czartoryski, a Polish noble active in the Russian government, and, above all, to Emperor Alexander I. Alexander showed a spirit of magnanimity towards the Poles by allowing the Polish troops that had fought against him under Napoleon to return home under arms and form the nucleus of a new Polish army. The Tsar himself was so Polonophile, at least at the beginning, that he risked his popularity among Russian patriots by hinting at the possibility of incorporating the territories of historical Lithuania into the Polish Kingdom. Small wonder then, that these hints aroused a wave of Russophile enthusiasm among many Poles, and that the intellectual life of the new kingdom was strongly permeated by Slavophile ideas.

The chief intellectual leader of this newborn Polish Slavophilism was undoubtedly Stanisław Staszic. In his case, however, Slavophilism stemmed not from a fundamental anti-Westernism, but merely from a political option based on geopolitical considerations and supported to a certain extent by a deep disillusionment with the Western attitudes towards Poland.[16]

Other Polish Slavophiles of the Congress Kingdom went much further and idealized Slavdom as a separate civilization—one superior to that of the West, and destined to develop differently, on the basis of an agrarian economy, religion, and strong communal ties. Some of them, like bishop Jan Paweł Woronicz, or the sentimentalist writer Kazimierz Brodziński, saw the purest embodiment of the Slavic type in the Poles, but others—like the historian, Ignacy Benedykt Rakowiecki, an expert on old Russian laws and the editor of *Russian Justice* (*Russkaia pravda*)—chose a strongly Russophile tendency. The most extreme representative of the latter position was the young enthusiast of the Slavic archeology and folklore, Zorian Dołęga-Chodakowski (Adam Czarnocki, 1784–1825). His treatise *On Slavdom Before Christianity* (*O słowiańszczyźnie przed chrześcijaństwem;* 1818) anticipated many ideas of the Russian Slavophiles, including the idealization of the Russian village commune and the negative stereotype of Poland as a hopelessly "Latinized" Slavic country.

However, pro-Russian Slavophilism had no chance to make the Poles loyal subjects of the Russian emperor, even if crowned as king of the Constitutional Kingdom of Poland. Polish patriots felt themselves to be citizens of an invisible *res publica,* ruled by an informal "moral government," composed of the most authoritative representatives of the national elite in the three parts of the partitioned country. Their radicalism drew strength from Romanticism, as a current of thought stressing the power of rebellious feelings and contemptuously rejecting the idea of a "reasonable reconciliation with reality." It was symbolic that the most famous theorist of Polish Romanticism, Maurycy Mochnacki, became an outstanding ideologist of the left wing of the November Insurrection of 1830.

In a book written on the eve of the insurrection Mochnacki (who was, by the way, the scion of a Polonized Ruthenian family) called Polish literature of his time an organ of national self-consciousness, a proof that Poles "had recognized themselves in their essence."[17] He assumed that Polish literary culture would help to unite all lands of historical Poland, including Ukraine; the "Borderlands" were expected to produce distinctive regional traditions in Polish literature, contributing thereby to the enrichment of the Polish national spirit.[18] This proved to be an extremely successful cultural program: the literature of partitioned Poland willingly accepted the task of promoting national consciousness, performed this brilliantly, and deserved to be seen as a most powerful factor of national unity.

The consequences of the defeat of the Insurrection of 1830–1831 were disastrous for Poland's political existence, but favorable for the development of Polish thought. The Kingdom of Poland lost its constitution, its separate parliamentary government, and even its name, so that Poland disappeared once more from the map of Europe. Almost 10,000 of the defeated insurgents, among them the major part of Poland's intellectual elite, chose political exile—mostly in France—something which came to be known as the "Great Emigration." Political freedom, direct confrontation with the West, and the urgent need to settle accounts with the painful events of the recent past, caused these people to engage in an ardent debate about "the Polish question." This was not merely a political debate; it revolved around such problems as Poland's self-definition, the meaning of its past, and the universal significance of its historical mission. It thus gave rise to a series of philosophical and religious controversies. Despite the fact that different conditions existed in Poland, all of these emigré controversies greatly influenced the intellectual life of the homeland.

One of the major themes in these passionate discussions was the problem of "Poland and the West." It is no exaggeration to say that this problem divided the Poles of the Romantic Epoch almost as deeply as it did the Russians.[19] If the division was somewhat less visible in Poland than in Russia this was due to the greater differentiation and the more articulate politicization of Polish thought during this epoch. In comparison with Russia, Poland produced more variants of both Westernism and anti-Westernism, both on the Left and on the Right. For practical reasons, traditional political divisions between Left and Right often overshadowed different civilizational options.

In the beginning, the main issue in the Polish Slavophile-Westernizer debate was the problem of republicanism versus monarchism, that is, of the alleged anomaly of the ancient democracy of the gentry, and of the heritage of the Polish Enlightenment. In this debate Polish Westernizers were politically organized in the emigré party of constitutional monarchists, led by Prince Adam Czartoryski, who headed the insurrectionary government in 1831. His name symbolized the continuity of the progressive tradition of eighteenth-century reformers, those who had paved the way for the Constitution of May 3rd. As a result his party was often referred to as "the party of the Third of May." The opposite camp, deeply critical of the May 3rd Constitution and of the entire Enlightenment tradition, found the best spokesman in the great historian Joachim Lelewel, chief representative of the Left in the insurrectionary government.

According to Lelewel's historical theory, democratic-republican principles were inherent in ancient Slavic communalism, and, as such, belonged to the common heritage of all Slavic nations, as distinct from the heritage of the West. He put special emphasis on the existence of a republican tradition in Russia, exemplified by the flourishing city-republics of Novgorod and Pskov, and spoke with great sympathy of the Decembrists who had tried to restore this "ancient Russian freedom."

On the whole, however, Russia for him was a sad example of a Slavic country in which the democratic and republican traditions of ancient Slavdom had been most cruelly suppressed by absolutism, deeply alien and hostile to the Slavic nature of the Russian people. The case of Poland was entirely different: here the Slavic principles had been weakened by "Latinism" (i.e., Western feudalism and Catholicism), but had later reemerged and reestablished themselves in the form of the "gentry democracy." True, the ancient Slavic freedom was confined in it to one estate alone. Nevertheless, Lewelel argued, the natural tendency of the "gentry democracy" was to expand freedom, not to restrict it. If this truly Slavic tendency did not prevail and result in the full democratization of the Commonwealth, it was the fault of the kings, who never got rid of monarchical leanings, and of the magnates, who distorted the egalitarian principles of the gentry.

Lelewel's final conclusions as to the legacy of the Polish past sounded very optimistic, even boastful. Poland had nothing to learn from the West. On the contrary, the contemporary West, decayed as it was, should learn from Poland.

In his idealization of the old Sarmatian Commonwealth Lelewel attached great importance to its multiethnic and, so to say, "multicultural" character. In this respect, too, the gentry democracy served him as a model for a future Poland, seen by him as a nation where "no differences would exist among the peoples: Polish, Lithuanian, German, Samogitian, Ruthenian, of which it is composed."[20] He overlooked the fact that despite this original indifference toward language and ethnicity, the culture of the gentry had undergone a process of homogenization, resulting in a homogeneous culture of "Sarmatianism." And it did not occur to him that political awakening of the peasant population of the former Commonwealth might result in consolidating the ethno-linguistic differences within it and thus give birth to new nations.

A similar error was made, as a rule, by those Polish democrats of the period who tried to modernize their nation on the French model. They were fairly united in their support for the integration of the historic territories of the Commonwealth, combatting all tendencies not only towards separatism but even towards regionalism, and after the emancipation and education of serfs they expected swift results in Polonization. Like Lewelel, they despised the May 3rd Constitution but, nonetheless, the unitarist tendency in their national ideology was basically in accord with the political thinking of the eighteenth-century Party of Reform. The Revolutionary Manifesto of the

Cracow Uprising of 1846—an uprising led by a romantic revolutionary and a passionate critic of the Enlightenment, Edward Dembowski—proclaimed the ideal of an integrated and unified democratic nation within the frontiers of 1772.[21] Thus, it fully disregarded the autonomous status of Lithuania. The Manifesto further stressed this by a significant change in the national arms from which the Lithuanian Chase (warrior on horse) was eliminated, now leaving the entire space of the emblem to the Polish White Eagle.

The opponents of the democratic camp, the constitutional monarchists of the Party of the Third of May, also tried to deduce their political position from the lessons of Polish history. The historian who provided them with the best arguments was Karol Hoffman. He was a staunch Westernizer, believing in the universal laws of historical development and resolutely rejecting Lelewel's thesis about the historical uniqueness and particular value of the communal institutions of ancient Slavdom. People, he maintained, are basically the same everywhere; the so-called "national spirit" is a product of changing historical circumstances, and by no means an independent, irreducible factor of historical development. Western feudalism—in the sense of a hierarchy within the nobility—and absolutism were normal phases of historical evolution, while the Polish "gentry democracy" was a historical anomaly, a deviation from the norm resulting from retarded development. Its final result was the gradual dissolution of the state. Royal power had no chance to become stronger; the overwhelming domination of the nobility over all other estates killed the embryonic growth of Polish cities, thus bringing about steadily increasing economic backwardness.

The emphasis on the link between strong monarchical power and the development of cities was an important element in the Westernizing liberalism of Czartoryski's followers. Like the architects of the May 3rd Constitution, they strongly believed that a future independent Poland would need a powerful enlightened bourgeoisie. The most colorful figure among them was one of the first Polish Fourierists, Jan Czyński—a converted Jew (from a Frankist family)—who cherished the idea that Polish Jews could be transformed into patriotic Polish burghers, and propagated this belief in his journal, *The Echo of the Polish Cities*.[22]

However, the Polish controversy over the West did not boil down to a debate about the respective values of Polish republicanism and Western monarchism. Polish democrats were increasingly aware that the overthrow of the reactionary Holy Alliance would require a deep social revolution, as opposed to merely political change. Of course, this was bound to profoundly influence the content of democratic anti-Westernism. To put it briefly, political anti-Westernism, critical of the eighteenth-century program of political reforms, was replaced by a socioeconomic anti-Westernism, stressing the possibility—and necessity—of avoiding industrialization and bourgeoisification on the Western model.

The most vocal in emphasizing this point were the Polish agrarian socialists, Stanisław Worcell and Zenon Świętosławski, founders of the "Communes of the Polish People," an organization whose membership consisted mostly of exiles of peasant origin who had fought in the November insurrection as simple illiterate soldiers.[23] Their first step was to cut themselves off from the views of the Polish Democratic Society (TDP), the most numerous and influential organization of the emigré Poles. The Democratic Society, they claimed, wanted to Westernize Poland by replacing its nobility with a "new aristocracy of money, potatoes, and cheese."[24] But at least the ancient nobility and the Catholic Church had a glorious past; their ideals and achievement were incomparably higher than anything created, or dreamt of, in the bourgeois-Protestant world. On the whole, the leaders of the "Communes" saw Western capitalism as a much worse evil than feudalism. This led them to declare: "We are ready to cover Poland with our corpses in order to free it from the plague of industry and trade, in the sense of the contemporary commercial exploitation."[25]

In this manner the Polish romantic socialists of the 1830s anticipated the views of the Russian populists of the 1870s: they had the same image of capitalism—as social retrogression, the same program of avoiding it at all costs, and the same clear awareness that this amounted to choosing a non-Western way of development.

The emergence of a full-fledged socialist anti-Westernism exercised a catalytic influence on the radicals from the Democratic Society. At the beginning, the Lelewelian idealization of the old Slavic communalism served them merely as justification of their republicanism, and republicanism, in turn was understood by most of them as republicanism of the Western type, representing the ideals of the American and French Revolutions. (In this respect they greatly differed from the Slavophile republicanism of Lelewel). However, with the passage of time, their growing disappointment with post-revolutionary Europe, as well as their need to distance themselves from the apologists of bourgeois development (a need of which their socialist opponents made them clearly aware), pushed them toward attempting to present their "Slavic principles" as containing the embryos of agrarian socialism. The leader of the Cracow Uprising of 1846, Edward Dembowski, who was a Left-Hegelian and revolutionary socialist, saw the whole of Polish history as a dialectical progression of the Slavic spirit overcoming its self-alienation in "Latinism" and returning to itself on a higher level, through rediscovering its communal values.[26] Other theorists affiliated with the TDP developed the theme of the contrast between Poland and the West in a less speculative way. Thus, for instance, Jan K. Podolecki saw the Slavs—led by the Poles—as representing the principle of solidarity and the idea of a global village, as opposed to the principle of individualism which typified the urban civilization of the West.[27] General Ludwik Mierosławski, a Polish revolutionary well known in the West for his activities and publications, was equally convinced that the program of the TDP was in accordance with ancient Slavic communalism, and that it had nothing in common with a repetition of the errors of the West. The assertion that Poland needed a strong bourgeoisie of its own aroused him to vigorous resistance. He claimed that the lack of a native bourgeoisie was a peculiar privilege of Poland, one which enabled it to skip the transitional phases of development and to introduce at once an unlimited sovereignty of the people, that is, democracy extended to the sphere of economic relations. He saw Poland as the purest incarnation of Slavic principles, and as the natural leader of all nations of Eastern Europe. This view, however, characteristically enough did not prevent him from praising the Russian peasant commune as a precious, albeit fossilized, relic of the common heritage of Slavdom.

It is justified to say that in the 1840s anti-Westernism was more widespread among Polish emigrés than Westernism. The latter had influential followers only among the liberal-conservative monarchists from Czartoryski's party; all groups to the left of it were vying with each other in anti-Westernism. Especially interesting and characteristic (although not typical in the sense of "representing the average") was the position of the greatest Polish poet, Adam Mickiewicz. In his lectures on Slavic literature in the Collège de France (1840–1844), lectures which greatly impressed Herzen and some of the Russian Slavophiles,[28] he managed to combine a truly Spenglerian vision of "the decline of the West" with revolutionary millenarism and a messianic conception of three chosen nations: the Jews, the French, and the Slavs. He condemned the bourgeois West (from a conservative-romantic standpoint) for its rationalism and atomistic individualism, and extolled the Slavs as faithful to the communal spirit—"not infected by rationalism, not demoralized by industrialization,"[29] retaining their spiritual and moral unity, capable of genuine enthusiasm and, therefore, best prepared to serve as a vessel for a "new revelation." He made it clear that he praised France as an *exceptional* Western nation—the only one which had preserved its "barbarian freshness." The Slavs, he proclaimed, did not need French engineers, industrialists, encyclopedists, and trade agents;[30] what they needed was the "holy fire" which burned in the breasts of the French saints, knights, revolutionaries of 1793, and soldiers of the Napoleonic army.

In this manner revolutionary zeal and a retrospective Slavophile utopia mixed together into a powerful chiliastic vision, resolutely condemning the decadent, bourgeois West. In Mickiewicz's view the nations of the West (apart from France) had exhausted their vitality. After the great God-inspired lawgivers had come legitimists and lawyers; "spiritual power" had been replaced by parliamentary discussion, bearing witness to a lack of inner strength; the bureaucratized Church had ceased to have contact with Heaven. After the apostles and miracle-workers had come the theologians and casuists; after the great warriors had come the people who proclaimed the doctrine of peace and non-intervention: " . . . such a generation is always a sign of the decline of the human spirit. This is how the Greek world came to an end, and how the Western world is now declining."[31]

Let us try to identify the reasons of this anti-Western turn in the Polish thought on the eve of the revolutionary Springtime of the Peoples. One of these reasons was, of course, the agrarian character of the lands of partitioned Poland, their economic underdevelopment, as well as the peculiarities of Polish intellectual elite, which fully participated in the intellectual life of more developed countries, and was painfully aware of its responsibility for the freedom and progress of the nation. From this came the phenomenon of the "penitent gentry," who defined themselves as "intelligentsia," and spoke about their "debt to the people" and about the need for "going to the people." Their revolutionary ideas emerged at a time when purely "bourgeois" radicalism had been already discredited, when the so-called "demonstration effect" of the French Revolution was felt to be deeply disappointing, and when the capitalist system had already been severely criticized by socialist thinkers of the West. This gave rise to the temptation to define backwardness as a privileged position, and to look for embryos of the desired social regeneration in native heritage.

It can easily be seen that in this respect the situation of the Polish revolutionaries of the Romantic Epoch was similar to that of the Russian revolutionary populists of the second half of the century. But the other reasons for Polish romantic anti-Westernism were peculiar to Poland, bound up with the specific situation and specific tasks of Polish romantic nationalism.

The Polish independence movement of the Romantic Epoch struggled against the Holy Alliance of the three absolute monarchs—the main bulwark of European reaction. For that reason Poland (as Marx and Engels put it) became a "revolutionary nation," "a revolutionary part of Russia, Austria and Prussia,"[32] an ally of the revolutionary forces of Western Europe. Polish revolutionaries were deeply aware of this and took their revolutionary mission very seriously—as proof that their struggle was necessary for humankind, uniquely important for the universal progress. Poland, proclaimed Mickiewicz, "must initiate a new, better world, otherwise it makes no sense to struggle for her independence."[33]

In this way the Polish national cause was made inseparable from the commitment to a revolutionary destruction of the corrupt "old world," to be followed by a universal regeneration. It would be odd to associate such commitment with "Westernism." The existing bourgeois West was, after all, a part of the "old World," no less than the semifeudal monarchies of the

Holy Alliance. A "revolutionary nation," struggling for a deep transformation of the entire European Order, could not see its task as merely a modernization on the Western model. Revolutionary messianism, as a part of national self-definition, forcefully suggested that its bearers represented completely new principles and new, infinitely higher values.

Finally, we must not forget that the Polish revolutionaries of the Romantic Epoch saw Poland's historical destiny as common to all peoples of the former Commonwealth. They stubbornly hoped that the Ukrainian and Belarusian peasants would join the Polish revolutionary movement and freely define themselves as "political Poles." Hence they could not define Polishness in exclusively Western terms, such as the "Latin civilization" (which could exclude even the Greek-rite Catholics). They wanted to set against Russian Panslavism an alternative concept of Slavdom. Mierosławski expressed this aspiration, defining Polish nationality as nothing less than "the proper, free and normal development of the Slavic civilization."[34] But a Slavic civilization, uniting the Western and Eastern Slavs, could not define itself, at that time at least, in terms of an unqualified Westernism. What had not been possible in the Sarmatian Commonwealth of the gentry, could not have become possible in the romantic dream of its restoration on a new popular basis.

References

1. See Milan Kundera, "The Tragedy of Central Europe," *New York Review of Books* 26 April 1984.
2. See Janusz Tazbir, "Stosunek do obcych w dobie baroku." In Zofia Stefanowska, ed., *Swojskość i cudzoziemszczyzna w dziejach kultury polskiej* [The Native and the Foreign in the History of Polish Culture] (Warsaw, 1973), p. 102. See also Janusz Tazbir, "Culture of the Baroque in Poland," in Antoni Mączak, et al., eds., *East-Central Europe in Transition* (Cambridge, 1985).
3. See Stanisław Orzechowski, *Wybór pism* (Wroclaw, 1970), pp. 43–45.
4. See Łukasz Opaliński, *De officiis* (1659), in Zbigniew Ogonowski, ed., *Filozofia i myśl społeczna XVII wieku* (Warsaw, 1979), vol. 1, pp. 48–50.
5. *Kronika polska, litewska, żmudzka i wszystkiej Rusi* (1582). It aroused vivid interest in Muscovy and was translated four times, fully or partially, into Russian (1668, 1673, 1682, and 1688). See *Istoriia polskoi literatury* (Moscow, 1968), vol. 1, p. 29 (chapter written by Liubov Viacheslavovna Razumovskaia and Boris Fedorovich Stakheev).
6. See Ogonowski, *Filozofia*, pp. 32–38 and Józef Ujejski, *Dzieje polskiego mesjanizmu*, (L'viv [Lwów], 1931), pp. 44–48. Dębołęcki's curious work, entitled *Wywód jedynowladnego państwa świata*, was published in 1633.
7. See Mate Mieses. *Z rodu żydowskiego. Zasłużone rodziny polskie krwi niegdyś żydowskiej* (Warsaw, 1991), pp. 21–24.
8. Jerzy Michalski, "Sarmatyzm a europeizacja Polski w XVII wieku" [Sarmatism and Europeanization of Poland in the 18th Century], in Stefanowska, *Swojskość*, p. 113.

9. Ibid., p. 144.
10. For a comprehensive analysis see Andrzej Walicki *The Age of Enlightenment and the Birth of Modern Nationhood: Polish Political Thought From the Noble Republicanism to Tadeusz Kościuszko* (Notre Dame, Indiana, 1989).
11. Ernest Gellner, *Nations and Nationalism* (Ithaca and London, 1983), p. 138.
12. See Michał Wielhorski, *O przywróceniu dawnego rządu według pierwiastkowych Rzeczypospolitej ustaw* [On the Restoration of the Former Government According to the Original Statuses of the Republic], 1775.

Rousseau wrote his *Considérations sur le gouvernement de Pologne* on the request of the Bar confederates, on the basis of the detailed "Tableau du gouvernement de Pologne," prepared for him by Wielhorski.

13. See Walicki, *The Age of Enlightenment*, pp. 22–26.
14. Karl Marx, *Przyczynki do historii kwestii polskiej (Beitrage zur Geschichteder Polnischen Frage). Manuscripts of 1863–1864* (Warsaw, 1971), pp. 151–52.
15. The co-author of this pamphlet was Kościuszko's Secretary, Józef Pawlikowski. For anew, critical edition of this text see Emanuel Halicz (ed.), *Czy Polacy mogą się wybić na niepodległość?* (Warsaw, 1967).
16. He described his motives as follows: "Western Europe permitted the partition of Poland, and so she must serve one more powerful; she neglected to find an ally in the Poles, and she will have them, incorporated in Slavdom, as lords. The die is already cast. Let us unite with Russia. We will take might from her, and let her take enlightenment from us." (See Kajetan Koźmian, *Pamiętniki*, [Warsaw, 1907], p. 79).

The manifesto of Staszic's Panslavism was his treatise *Myśli o równowadze politycznej w Europie* [Reflections on the Political Balance in Europe], 1815. It argued that the Slavs had a political right to unite the peoples of Europe under their hegemony, for it was they—both the Russians and the Poles—who had for centuries been the sole defense of Europe against the Asiatic hordes. It did not, however, see the Slavs as bearers of a qualitatively different civilization. On the contrary, their ascension was reguarded as the next phase in an essentially Eurocentric universal progress.

17. Maurycy Mochnacki, *O literaturze polskiej w wieku XIX*, in Mochnacki, *Pisma wybrane* (Warsaw, 1957), p. 215.
18. In Mochnacki's time this program of expressing and shaping sub-national regional identities was successfully realized by the so-called "Ukrainian School" in Polish literature.
19. I stressed this point in my different works on Polish thought of this period and in the book *Philosophy and Romantic Nationalism: The Case of Poland*. Oxford 1982. For a consistent and convincing presentation of this view see also Jerzy Jedlicki, "Polskie nurty ideowe lat 1790–1863 wobec cywilizacji Zachodu" [Polish intellectual currents of 1790–1863 and Western Civilization], in Stefanowska, op. cit., pp. 186–231. Jedlicki's book *Jakiej cywilizacji Polacy potrzebują?* (Warsaw, 1988) is a monograph on the "civilizational options" concerning economic development in Polish thought from the Enlightenment to Positivism.
20. Joachim Lelewel. *Polska, Dzieje i rzeczy jej*, vol. 20 (Poznań, 1864), p. 558.
21. See Tadeusz Łepkowski, *Rozważania o losach polskich* (London, 1987), p. 62, Cf. idem, "Poglądy na jedno-i wieloetniczność narodu w XIX wieku," in Stefanowska, ed., *Swojskość*, p. 232.
22. See Artur Eisenbach, *Wielka Emigracja wobec kwestii żydowskiej 1832–1849* (Warsaw, 1976), pp. 268–71.

23. One of these "Communes, composed of the members of the gentry, named itself the "Commune of Humań." Humań was the place of a bloody Ukrainian peasant *jacquerie* in the eighteenth century; hence choosing this name was to symbolize a penitence for the wrongdoing of the Polish gentry. (See Peter Brock, *Polish Revolutionary Populism: A Study in Agrarian Socialist Thought From the 1830s to the 1850s*. [Toronto and Buffalo, 1977], p. 25).

It is interesting to note that this also implied that the peasants from Humań were seen as a part of "the Polish people." It would be utterly ahistorical to interpret it as a nationalistic desire to deprive the Ukrainian of their ethnic identity. It reflected only the fact that the terms "Polish people" and "Polish nation" were used by then as political notions, referring to the population of the former Polish state, regardless of ethnicity. Such use of these terms was not characteristic of Polish patriots only. Wiktor Sukiennicki has rightly stressed that even in the text of the Treaty of Vienna the name "Poles" refers to the whole population of the former Commonwealth. See W. Sukiennicki, *East Central Europe During World War I*, vol. 1 (New York, 1984), pp. 12 and 28.

24. See Hanna Temkinowa (ed.), *Lud Polski-Wybór dokumentów* (Warsaw, 1957), pp. 70–1.

25. Ibid., p. 116.

26. See Walicki, *Philosophy and Romantic Nationalism*, pp. 206–225.

27. He wrote: "The social idea of the Slavs is the village, village life, while the city, *civitas*, is the idea of the Western heir of the Roman Empire." Jan K. Podolecki, *Wybor pism* (Warsaw, 1955), p. 6.

28. See Andrzej Walicki, "Adam Mickiewicz's Paris Lectures and Russian Slavophilism," in Walicki, *Russia, Poland, and Universal Regeneration: Studies on Russian and Polish Thought of the Romantic Epoch* (Notre Dame, Indiana, 1991), pp. 107–157.

The importance of Mickiewicz's Paris lectures for the understanding of both Mickiewicz's *oeuvre* and Polish Romanticism in general was stressed in the pioneering works of Wiktor Weintraub: "Adam Mickiewicz, the Mystic-Politician," in *Harvard Slavic Studies*, vol. 1 (Cambridge, Mass., 1953), and *Literature and Prophecy* (S'Gravenhage, 1959). Before Weintraub, this extremely rich ideological document was the most neglected part of Mickiewicz's legacy. Its heterodox mysticism was too embarrassing for orthodox Catholics, and no less embarrassing for positivistically minded or Marxist scholars.

29. Adam Mickiewicz, *Dziela* (Warsaw, 1955), vol. 10, p. 315.

30. Ibid., vol. 11, pp. 338–39.

31. Ibid., p. 336.

32. Karl Marx, Friedrich Engels, *Collected Works*, vol. 6, p. 373. For a detailed presentation of Marx's and Engels's view on the "Polish Question" see my *Philosophy and Romantic Nationalism*, part IV, ch. II: "Marx, Engels, and the Polish Question" (pp. 358–91).

33. A. Mickiewicz, *Dziela wszystkie*, vol. 16 (Warsaw, 1932), p. 341.

34. L. Mierosławski, *De la nationalité polonaise dans l'équilibre européen* (Paris, 1856), p. IX.

LECTURE II

Organic Work and Civilizational Options

Varieties of Organic Work before 1863

In contrast to the emigrés, who had nothing to lose and everything to gain, the Poles in their homeland were less susceptible to revolutionary hopes and Messianic dreams. As a result, they exhibited a much greater tolerance toward the idea of a peaceful and gradual "bourgeois progress." The mainstream intelligentsia in the Congress Kingdom after 1831 was practically minded, and was neither anti-Western nor enthusiastically committed to Westernism. Nonetheless, anti-Westernism was a living issue in the lands of partitioned Poland. What was at stake was the agrarian character of the country. It was natural that anti-Westernism characterized the ideologies of the extreme agrarian Left, similar to those in the emigration; suffice it to mention here the Left-Hegelian revolutionary socialism of Edward Dembowski, or revolutionary millenarism of Father Piotr Ściegienny.[1] Another variant of anti-Westernism, unknown in the emigration, was flourishing in the ideologies of the agrarian Right. Its most extreme representative, Count Henryk Rzewuski, developed his anti-Western, pro-Russian feelings to the point of bordering on national apostasy. Poland, he argued, had proved unable to resist the corrupting influence of the West, and had betrayed its own Sarmatian tradition, thereby ceasing to be a living, organic nation. Its best national values, embodied in the nobility, were threatened from within and could survive only under the protection of the powerful Russian Empire, the most reliable defender of the Old World.[2]

Rzewuski's position, although rather unique in its extremism, reflected a tendency toward conciliation with Russia which was at that time quite common among the wealthy Polish landowners in Ukraine. The situation in the Congress Kingdom was, of course, different, but even there the landowners—threatened by the enfranchisement of the peasants—tended to embrace a strongly anti-Western stance. Thus, for instance, Adam Krzysztopór (Tomasz Potocki), an influential leader of the landed gentry, took alarm at the prospect of the compulsory expropriation that haunted the West in the form of socialism and that was coming to the East in the form of the idea of dispossessing the legitimate owners of their land. This danger, he claimed, originated in the West and resistance to it was the sacred mission of the Slavic East.[3] Similar ideas were developed by Józef Gołuchowski, a philosopher and disciple of Schelling, who, after the revolutionary events of 1846–1848, concentrated his efforts on finding a solution to the peasant question. He claimed that the West (except England) had embraced the fatal principle of distributive justice ("take away from one and give to another"); this made it imperative for the Polish landlords to give up aping Western countries and to cling instead to the "native Slavic policy."[4] As a philosophical foundation for this policy he proposed the conception of nation as an organic whole. Inequality, he argued, is a necessary condition of organic wholeness; equalizing tendencies can emerge only in an atomized society. As a good example of an organic society he pointed to Russia, contrasting it favorably with the decaying atomized West. He found warm words for Russian serfdom, describing it as an "organic" institution, and praised highly the Russian peasant commune, stressing its stabilizing function in rural life.[5] He made it clear, however, that in the Congress Kingdom— where the Napoleonic Code guaranteed the personal freedom of the peasants and established their relations with the landlords on the basis of contracts— any introduction of the commune would be undesirable, as this would weaken the position of the wealthy villagers and increase the egalitarian appetites of the poor peasantry.

The Agricultural Association, a patriotic organization of the landowners of the Congress Kingdom headed by Count Andrzej Zamoyski, wanted to solve the peasant question on the English model.[6] This meant treating all land as the exclusive property of the gentry, and thus transforming peasants into tenants who would pay for the use of land in cash—a solution which would abolish *corvée* and stimulate the development of commodity production. From the point of view of the peasants, this programmatically Occidentalist solution was similar to Gołuchowski's position, but the differences should not be neglected. Gołuchowski's "Slavophilism" represented a variant of agrarian conservatism, while Zamoyski's Anglophile program put more emphasis on the general capitalist modernization of the country.

Aleksander Wielopolski, the Polish statesman who in 1862 assumed the duties of head of the civilian administration of the Congress Kingdom, had a similar program on the agrarian question. He tried to realize it as a part of a series of ambitious reforms, with the aim of implementing a consistent, though socially conservative modernization of the country. He unfortunately failed to win Zamoyski's support, let alone the confidence of broader patriotic circles. This was the sad result of his arrogant disregard of popular emotions, stemming from the conviction that, as he put it, "much can be done *for* the Poles, but nothing with their participation." As a result of this attitude, his policy—although it won several concessions from the Tsar— proved to be a miscalculation and unintentionally brought about the desperate uprising of 1863–1864. This was an uprising whose aim was described by one of its leaders not as material victory, but as strengthening the morale of the nation through shedding "a river of blood" and thus making impossible any "rotten compromise" with Russia.[7]

The defeat of the uprising closed the "epoch of Romanticism." In order to complete its picture it should be stressed that anti-Westernism, combined with both revolutionary and conservative politics, coexisted by then with a strong current of "organic work," which concentrated on the problems of the economic and social modernization of the country and took for granted that this meant development on the Western model. This current of thought was especially strong in the Prussian part of Poland—the grand Duchy of Poznań. The leaders of the movement for organic work in Poznania were speculative philosophers, August Cieszkowski and Karol Libelt, who tried to transform Hegelianism into a "philosophy of action" and to combine organic work with an active commitment to struggle for national independence. They elaborated several impressive schemes for conscious purposeful action—programs which proved to be quite successful in mobilizing, organizing and directing the energy of the nation.[8] They wanted to initiate economic developments, to accelerate economic growth, and to make it serve national goals, as distinct from the interests of partitioning powers. Hence they could not be satisfied with the laissez-faire model. This explains why classical economic liberalism could not find faithful adherents in nineteenth-century Poland.

The Positivist Epoch and the Turn toward Westernization

The post-Romantic epoch in Polish intellectual history, stretching from 1864 to the 1890s, is usually called the epoch of Positivism. Its first decade saw the liquidation of the relative autonomy of the Congress Kingdom and the disappearance of the "Polish question" from the agenda of European diplomacy. Polish society reacted to this by a sharp depoliticization of its national aspirations. The ideal of political independence came to be seen as a romantic fantasy which had to be abandoned, temporarily at least, for the sake of national survival. It was agreed that in order to survive, the Poles must modernize themselves—economically, socially and intellectually. This program of civilizational or cultural "work at the foundations" (a new version of the old idea of "organic work") was embraced by a group of able journalists who attacked romantic illusions in the name of Positivism. The most important among them were Adam Wiślicki, the editor of *Przegląd Tygodniowy* (*Weekly Review*), Aleksander Świętochowski, and the novelist Bolesław Prus.

The Positivists' ascendancy in the Congress Kingdom was, of course, a victory of modernizing Westernism. Culturally and ideologically it was a radical Westernism, wholeheartedly committed to Western scientism, supporting a thorough secularization of education and culture, and strongly critical of the conservative mentality and class egoism of the landowning gentry. Economically, however, it was a Westernism with qualifications. Its positive heroes were the intelligentsia rather than the "captains of industry," and its image of "organic work" was modelled on disinterested public service rather than on the liberal conception of furthering worthy private interests in a spontaneously regulated civil society. Hence they took from Spencer, their favorite thinker, the ideas of organicism and evolutionism, but rejected his unbending "laissez-faire" position; they listened rather to J. S. Mill's arguments against unrestricted competition, and were ready to learn even from the socialists. Characteristically, their attitude towards capitalists and the bourgeoisie as a whole was rather suspicious. Apart from general distrust, there were local reasons for such an attitude: the bourgeoisie of the Congress Kingdom was composed of Germans and non-assimilated Jews, whose loyalty to Poland was often suspect. The ethnic tensions in industry were increased by the fact that the workers were mostly Polish, while the foremen were mostly German. For that reason Adam Wiślicki was extremely cautious about the benefits of quick industrialization; he tried instead to mobilize social support for independent small producers, and aimed at transforming Polish proletarians into independent artisans.[9] Moderate Positivists, whose best spokesman was Bolesław Prus, were more supportive of industrialization. They stressed, however, the urgent need to Polonize the bourgeoisie of the Kingdom, and thus to redress the unhealthy relation between, to use Prus' expression, the "regulating organ" (that is, non-Polish capitalists and financiers) and the "productive class" (that is, Polish workers) in the native industry.[10] Świętochowski, although also aware of these problems, was convinced that industrialization, despite all its dangers, was for the Poles the only way to active membership in universal civilization, and thus was necessary to ensure their national survival. From his point of view, the lack of political independence was not necessarily a disadvantage: incorporation into an alien state, he argued, could be a blessing because it could free the nation from the burden of having to develop a foreign policy and from military ambitions, thus enabling it to concentrate fully on economic and civilizational progress. In the case of Poland there was an additional advantage: incorporation into the Russian Empire opened the vast Russian and Asian markets to Polish industrial products, thereby greatly contributing to the rapid industrialization of the Congress Kingdom which took place after the emancipation of the peasants in 1864. In Świętochowski's eyes this seemed more important than the Russification of the Polish schools, the severe censorship, and even the restrictions put on the usage of the Polish language.

Nevertheless, Świętochowski cannot be treated as an ideologist of the bourgeoisie and an uncritical advocate of capitalist development. He was a typical ideologist of the intelligentsia, whom he extolled as the only social force representing the general interest of the nation. His belief in the benefits of industrialization was much greater than his confidence in capitalists, hence he was tempted to think about a non-capitalist industrialization. This led him to conclude a tactical alliance in 1886 with the first Polish Marxists.

The Positivists can be described as occupying a centrist position in the intellectual life of the Congress Kingdom. Their right-wing opponents consisted of two groups, which differed greatly from one another.[11] The first group was composed of agrarian conservatives, who saw themselves as defenders of traditional "Polishness," embodied in the landowning gentry. Since the Russifying policies of the Russian authorities left no room for Slavophile tendencies, they stressed Poland's Western heritage. In practice, however, this heritage was reduced by them to a traditionalist Catholicism, that is, to a position from which it was possible to resist new trends in Western civilization such as bourgeois liberalism and socialism. Accordingly, the conservatives wanted Poland to remain an agrarian country, faithful to traditional Catholic values. They were critical of industrialization in general, saying it brought about social atomization. They were critical of Polish industrialization in particular, since they saw it as strengthening the position of alien elements in national life. Their practical program was "organic work," under the guidance of truly Polish and Christian ideals. With respect to "alien elements," especially Jews, this meant religious and cultural assimilation (with intermarriage as a means to this end), while with respect to the peasants it involved their cultural "ennoblement," that is, educating them in the spirit of the traditional values of the gentry. (As is known, Henryk Sienkiewicz's novels made this program amazingly successful.) Naturally, from this point of view Positivists were seen as corrupting the Poles by spreading alien, immoral doctrines among them. They were also seen as enemies of the Church and of traditional Polish values, and, finally, as reckless supporters of an unrestrained industrialization which paved the way for the rule of alien "plutocrats" and an alienated, secular intelligentsia, thus undermining the moral cohesion of the nation.

The other group criticized the Positivists from right-wing positions and was composed of radically anti-semitic nationalists, whose main ideologist was Jan Jeleński, the editor of *Rola* (Soil). They had no prestige among the progressive intelligentsia, and no good connections with the traditionalist landowners, but were vividly responsive to the ideological needs of the Polish petty-bourgeoisie, who saw the Jews as their main rivals. Hence, Jeleński's program was "organic work" combined with economic warfare against the Jews. It therefore supported only such forms of industrial development that served the interests of ethnic Poles. It should be stressed, however, that there was no biological racism in this position. Jeleński accused both Positivists and Conservatives of excessive tolerance of Jews, but readily conceded that before 1864 philosemitic attitudes had been justified. This was the case, he argued, because the slogan "Poles of Mosaic faith" made sense in a situation when the Poles were concentrating on the struggle for national independence and the Jews, heavily oppressed by the Russians, could be their natural allies. Now, however, Polish national aspirations had been geared to economic development, and the economic struggle had become, indeed, a struggle for national survival; in this sphere Polish and Jewish interests were opposite and irreconcilable.[12]

The left-wing critics of Positivism, the first Polish Marxists, also deserve some attention in the present context. To be sure, this is so not because they were Marxists, but, rather, because of their interesting deviation from the Marxist orthodoxy of their time—a deviation which resulted from their attempts to grasp the specificity of the socioeconomic development of an underdeveloped capitalist country.

In the ideology of the first Polish Marxists two different tendencies are to be distinguished: a social-revolutionary and a social-democratic one.[13] The first was prevalent in Ludwik Waryński's party *Proletariat* (founded in 1882). The second dominated the circle of Polish socialists in the Russian University of Warsaw, headed by Stanisław Krusiński. Generally speaking, the Social Revolutionaries, who closely collaborated with the Russian populist party *Narodnaia volia* (The People's Will), put an emphasis on the role of the "subjective factor" in history, while the Social Democrats insisted on the economic conditions for a socialist revolution. Owing to this, the Social Democrats took a consistently Westernizing position, stressing the necessity of passing through "the capitalist phase" and treating the Warsaw Positivists as welcome allies. The standpoint of the Social Revolutionaries was diametrically opposite: they believed that the Polish workers could bring about a socialist revolution without waiting for the maximal development of the capitalist system in Poland; hence they treated the liberal bourgeoisie (represented by the Positivists) as their direct enemies and looked for allies among the poor peasantry. The maturity of objective economic conditions, they argued, was not everything; no less important was the ripeness of subjective conditions, that is, of the class consciousness, political experience, and militant spirit of the masses. The historical experience of more advanced Western countries made the Polish bourgeoisie too afraid of the revolutionary potential of the workers to be able to perform any progressive historical mission; on the other hand, the Polish proletariat, having learned from class struggle in the West, was more immune to bourgeois illusions, more susceptible to socialist ideas, that is, more mature than Western workers had been at a comparable stage of economic development. Similarly, the Polish peasants were expected to transform their hatred of feudal exploitation into the hatred of all forms of exploitation, including capitalism, thus becoming a powerful ally of the proletarian revolution. Polish workers were to start the revolution by accomplishing the tasks of a bourgeois-democratic transformation, but without surrendering political power to the bourgeoisie; soon afterwards they were to set about their own, proletarian tasks—to bring about a socialist transformation of society. The leadership in the revolutionary struggle was to belong to a well-organized, conspiratorial socialist party; after the victory of the revolution this party was to institutionalize itself as the main organ of political power in the new state. The essence of this power was described as the "dictatorship of the proletariat."[14]

As can be seen from the above, the theoretical controversy between the first Polish Marxists was similar to the Russian controversy between Plekhanov's group (whose standpoint was very close to that of the Polish "Social Democrats") and the ideologists of *Narodnaia volia*. We should not conclude from this that the Polish "Social Revolutionaries" were simply influenced by Russian revolutionary populists, and, therefore, that their Marxism, contaminated by heterogeneous elements, was simply "less Marxist" than the Marxism of the Social Democrats. In contradistinction to the Russian controversies of the beginning of the 1880s, the Polish dispute between "Social Revolutionaries" and "Social Democrats" was a controversy *within* Marxism. If we look at it from the perspective of the later development of Marxist thought in Russia we can find in it an anticipation of some theoretical and ideological differences between Russian Bolsheviks and Mensheviks.

Apart from the Congress Kingdom (this name was widely used despite the efforts of the Russian authorities to substitute for it the term "Vistula Land" [Rus. *Privislianskii krai*, Pol. *Kraj Nadwiślański*]), Polish intellectual life flourished in Galicia, the Austrian part of partitioned Poland, which since 1867 had enjoyed the status of an autonomous province under Polish rule. Political affairs there were in the hands of the gentry conservatives, who called themselves "Stańczyks"—after the name of a patriotic royal jester who had become famous for his bitter criticism of the Polish national character.[15] Their ideology, elaborated by the so-called Cracow school in Polish historiography (Józef Szujski, Michał Bobrzyński, and others), stressed the need for inculcating into Poles a respect for governmental authority—a spirit of hierarchy and discipline—thereby freeing them from the fatal legacy of the anarchic freedom of the gentry democracy, and, also, of the irresponsible political romanticism of the times of national insurrections. Firmly convinced that the ultimate cause of Poland's ill fortunes was its deviation from the Western model of development, according to which the feudal liberties of the nobility should have been abrogated by a strong centralized monarchy, they liked to present themselves as Westernizers, helping Poles to overcome their anarchic Sarmatianism and its romantic continuations. They were bitterly critical of Polish history, and claimed that the Poles themselves should be blamed for the multiple disasters that fell to their lot. On the other hand, they were fond of pleasing both their compatriots and the Austrians by arguing that as a part of the Habsburg Empire the Poles could continue their historical mission of serving as a bastion of the Catholic West. For us, declared Szujski, Austria is not a dynasty, or a particular state; it represents "the question of Central Europe, the question of the Western civilization, which we are bound to serve."[16]

The historical synthesis elaborated by the Cracow School (of which Szujski's extremely negative view of the Polish "gentry democracy" was an important part) became very influential in Poland. The Cracow historians proved very successful in discrediting the republican-libertarian tradition of the "gentry democracy" and in setting against it the idea of a strong authoritarian government. They were equally successful in destroying within Polish minds the spell of Lelewel's romantic Slavophilism and in firmly establishing the thesis of the Western, or (more precisely) Latin character of Polish civilization. Their ideological legacy, combining a sharp critique of Polish national character with strongly authoritarian leanings, provided historical arguments for all supporters of stronger government in Poland. Their authority was often invoked for that purpose in the interbellum period and even in the Polish People's Republic.

For Poles steeped in the Romantic tradition, most of these ideas were provocative and deeply repulsive. Thus, for instance, Stefan Buszczyński, a belated apologist of the insurrection of 1863, wrote a lengthy (three volumes!) refutation of the Stańczyks' interpretation of Polish history, giving it a self-explanatory title *Defence of a Vilified Nation* (1888). He boldly attacked the "Westernism" of the Cracow historians, claiming that the calling of Poland had always been different and nobler than the calling of the West. Poland saw its mission in peacefully uniting different tribes into a free nation while the West, the inheritor of the imperial tradition of predatory ancient Rome, devoted all its energy to building states, expanding through conquests and seeking only material power.[17] Poland's inability to compete with the West in the struggle for domination was the other side of its spiritual superiority. The romantic poet, Zygmunt Krasiński, was perfectly right in arguing that the Western road would have led the Poles to become "a market stall, and not a nation."[18]

Of course, such an approach to the problem of "Poland and the West" was deeply anachronistic in the last quarter of the nineteenth century. Both the Stańczyks and their critics discussed this problem as dealing with a historically-shaped *political* culture, while totally ignoring the aspect of

Westernization as modernization, the urgent need of catching up with Western Europe in *economic* terms. And, in the meantime, Galicia, ruled by the Stańczyks, was becoming one of the most backward provinces of the Empire. In the year 1888—the same year in which Buszczyński published his eulogy of the national character of the Poles—there appeared a book entitled *Galician Misery* (*Nędza Galicji*), which showed a truly frightening picture. In it, the Polish rulers of Galicia were accused of constantly asking for credits in Vienna while doing nothing to release and channel the productive energy of the population.[19] As a result, Galicia had fallen economically behind Bulgaria and Romania, let alone Hungary or Italy.[20] An average citizen of Galicia ate one-half of an average European's diet, and produced at the level of one-fourth of the average European productivity.[21]

The author of this book, Stanisław Szczepanowski, saw the only solution in the rapid industrialization of the province. But, interestingly enough, he wanted to achieve this goal by means of moral mobilization, thus making the cause of modernization dependent on a prior moral revival of the nation. This choice of strategy, so different from the usual methods of capitalist industrialization, stemmed from his unashamed romantic idealism, from his profound admiration for the Polish romantic philosophers and poets, whose works were for him the "Polish national revelation."[22] But there was also another reason: namely, Szczepanowski's assessment of the Polish national character. In his view, the type of *homo economicus* had not become widespread among Poles, and, therefore, their work depended primarily on moral motivation. This extraordinary sensitivity to moral incentives made Poles superior to other Europeans; on the other hand, however, it made their ethic too dependent on their moral condition, something which explained their extremely poor economic performance in a situation characterized by moral apathy and corruption. Thus, a morally motivated Pole was much better than a Western European, but a Pole lacking moral motivation, let alone one with a corrupted motivation, was much worse. Szczepanowski saw this as a corroboration of the old, Aristotelian observation that the corruption of the best results in the worst (*Corruptio optimi pessima*).

In this manner the pioneer of the industrialization of Galicia tried to combine the call for increased productivity with exalted praise of the pre-industrial features of the Polish mentality. He advocated quick industrialization, but, at the same time, cherished a strong anticapitalist bias. His conception of the Polish national character assumed that industrialization, in order to succeed in Poland, must appeal not to self-interest, but to idealistic enthusiasm and exalted patriotic feeling.

In spite of its obvious exaggerations, Szczepanowski's interpretation of the Polish national character contains an important element of truth—if not about the entire nation then at least about those Polish patriots who, like himself, remained imbued by the knightly traditions of the gentry. For three centuries civil society existed in Poland *in the public sphere* as the "political nation" of the gentry, while civil society as *bourgeois* society was conspicuously unrecognized and underdeveloped. Small wonder, then, that the Polish intelligentsia of gentry background had found it extremely difficult to accept bourgeois values. Even if they fully recognized the necessity of industrial development, they promoted industrial activity as a disinterested public service and patriotic duty, but never as a means of pursuing one's private interests.

The Changing Concept of the "Polish Nation"

An especially important contribution of the Positivist Epoch to the history of the "Polish idea" was a radical change in the very meaning of the term "Polish nation."

The generation of 1863, faithful to the romantic idealization of the old *Rzeczpospolita*, wanted to make the notion of the Polish nation as inclusive as possible. The best proof of this was the universal enthusiasm about the pro-Polish feelings among the Warsaw Jews, who actively participated in the patriotic manifestations on the eve of the uprising. They became immediately recognized as "Poles of the Mosaic persuasion" and were extolled in literature as heroic participants, or even organizers and leaders of the Polish struggle for independence. It is worthwhile to point out that this euphoria was not bound up with hoping that the Jews would convert to Catholicism. On the contrary: writers of that time propagated the idea of incorporating the Jews into the Polish nation without changing their religion and renouncing their ancient historic heritage. It became popular to stress the essential identity of the Jewish and Polish messianic hopes, to present Jews and Poles as "the two Israels," the two chosen nations whose mysterious alliance had now been sealed by blood and established forever.[23] The spread of the symbolic image of "the Jew with the cross," fighting together with the Poles under a common national flag, was accompanied by a conscious Old Testament stylization of Polish patriotism: Polish messianic poets were compared to Biblical prophets, freedom fighters were identified with the Maccabees, Poland was referred to as Zion, and Warsaw as Jerusalem.[24]

The attitude of the generation of 1863 toward the non-Polish nationalities of the former Commonwealth took the form of the "federal conception." The beginning of the insurrection was marked by a manifesto which called to arms the *three nations* of the Old Commonwealth: Poles, Lithuanians, and Ukrainians. Its banner showed the triune emblem of the federation composed of the Polish Eagle, the Lithuanian Chase, and the Ruthenian Archangel. In their dealings with the non-Polish nationalities of the former

Commonwealth, the insurgents used their respective languages, including Belarusian. In the negotiations between the Polish and Russian revolutionaries, which took place before the uprising, the Polish side agreed to respect the rights of democratic self-determination on the nationally mixed territories. At the same time, however, the Poles made clear that they hoped to influence events and to bring about a voluntary union of these nationalities with Poland, thus restoring the Old Commonwealth in the form of a free federation—one which would correct the fatal mistake of not recognizing the rights of the Ukrainian population. The best traditions of the Polish-Lithuanian Commonwealth were to be revived in a democratic federation composed of three basic units: Poland, Lithuania, and Ukraine.

The federal concept differed from the multicultural and unitarist concept by clearly recognizing that despite their close links with Poland, Lithuania and Ukraine were separate nations. This recognition, which was given somewhat grudgingly, was caused by several reasons, such as the progress of the Ukrainian national awakening, the growing influence of political theories defining nations in ethno-linguistic terms, and, last but not least, the increasing awareness among Poles themselves that the Polish language and Catholic religion were the most reliable elements of Polish national identity. Thus, the federal concept to the Poles who embraced it, did not imply membership in a multicultural federated nation but rather in a *Polish* nation which would be part of federation within which the distinctive national cultures of the former Commonwealth would be preserved and mutually respected. In this way, the federal option combined a nostalgia for the historic, multiethnic fatherland with an increased awareness of belonging to a culturally well-defined, Polish-speaking and Catholic nation. Owing to this, the January insurrection was more ardently and ostentatiously Catholic than previous Polish uprisings which had been either religiously neutral (as the uprising of 1830–1831), or even colored by a dose of anti-clericalism (as was the Kościuszko Uprising of 1794 and the Cracow Uprising of 1846). Recognizing the Ukrainians as a separate nation therefore had a double meaning. On the one hand it was, of course, the long delayed recognition of Ukrainian aspirations to nationhood, but on the other hand it recognized the difference between the Polish-speaking, Catholic population (Poles in the ethno-linguistic and cultural sense) and the Eastern Slavs.

As we can see, the federal concept was in fact the first important step toward abandoning the increasingly anachronistic idea of a single political nation. But it was still very far from a commitment to the ethno-linguistic criteria of nationality. For the generation of 1863 it was too difficult to imagine that Lithuanian or Ukrainian Poles might ever be treated as a national minority. It was expected that Lithuania and Ukraine would achieve separate nationhood as multicultural countries, allowing local Poles to define themselves as Lithuanians or Ukrainians of Polish culture, combining loyalty to their respective nations with continuing attachment to the Jagellonian tradition.[25]

The defeat of the uprising marked an end of many romantic illusions. The liquidation of the last remnants of the autonomy of the Kingdom of Poland, as well as its very name, put "Polishness" on the defensive and this, of course, favored the transition to the narrow, ethno-linguistic definition of the nation. An additional important factor in this process was the increased role and greater social visibility of German and Jewish elements in the rapidly developing capitalist industry of the Kingdom. The working class of the former Kingdom (now called by the Russian authorities "Vistula Land") constituted itself as a multiethnic body in which Polish speakers were in a subordinate position, subject to brutal treatment by German foremen and seeing themselves as exploited not so much by an impersonal "system" but, rather, by well-defined aliens—German and Jewish factory owners.

But there was also a positive side of this new situation. Twenty years after the uprising it became clear that it was wrong to fear that the emancipation of Polish peasants by the Russian authorities would make them loyal subjects of the Russian Empire, indifferent to national oppression. In fact the transformation of the semi-feudal peasantry into emancipated property owners consolidated their ethnic identity and thus created solid foundations for the new, ethno-linguistic nations. The Lithuanian peasants were becoming consciously Lithuanian, no longer willing to join the Polish insurrectionists (as they did, in contrast to Ukrainians, in 1863). But a similar process took place among the Polish peasants: their consciousness was becoming quickly "nationalized" through the increasing awareness of national oppression, elementary national needs (such as the use of native language in schools and offices) and, also, inevitable conflicts with the non-Polish petty bourgeoisie.

The first and most radical attempts to take these developments into account and to adequately reformulate the tasks of the nationalist Polish intellectuals appeared in 1886. One of them, published in the Warsaw populist weekly *Głos* (*Voice*), was entitled "Two Civilizations."[26] Its author, Jan Ludwik Popławski, claimed that Poles had always been divided into two nations—the historical "nation of the privileged" and the ethnic "nation of the peasantry." The former entered the last phase of its inevitable decline. The latter, representing a separate civilization, qualitatively different from the culture of the gentry, was the mainstay of national existence and the only basis for Poland's national and social regeneration.

The second manifesto of the new "peasantist" nationalism was "The Programmatic Sketches" published in Bolesław Wysłouch's *Przegląd Społeczny* (The Social Review).[27] The author went so far as to treat the tradition of the "political nation" of the gentry as mostly irrelevant for the modern, peasant-based nations of the former Commonwealth. In his view, the Polish-Lithuanian Union proved beneficial only for the gentry and did not lay foundation for a fusion of the two nations. Polish rule over Ukrainian and Belarusian peasants was just a foreign yoke which could not be justified by invoking the superiority of Polish culture. The principle of national self-determination should be applied to each ethno-linguistic nationality. This meant in practice that Poles had a right only to their "ethnographic territory," which would bring them some gains in the West (upper Silesia and Mazuria) and severe losses in the East. It was specifically insisted that L'viv (Lwów), in spite of its predominantly Polish character, should be left on the Ukrainian side.

Not surprisingly, mainstream public opinion in Poland proved to be unprepared to immediately accept these conclusions. Interestingly, negative reactions to the idea of an "ethnographic Poland" were especially strong on the left. Wysłouch's theses were subject to sharp criticism by Bolesław Limanowski, a non-Marxist socialist who was to become one of the founders of the Polish Socialist Party (PPS, founded in 1892). His concept of nationality minimized the role of "objective" criteria, such as ethnicity and language, underscoring instead the importance of "subjective" factors— common feelings, common historical memories, and loyalty to the values inherent in the country's historical tradition. He sharply distinguished between nation and state, as well as between "patriotism" and "nationalism," seeing the first as a legitimate expression of love and loyalty to one's nation, and the second as the immoral ideology and policy of the modern state, worshipping power for its own sake. He condemned ethnically-based nationalism (which he opposed to "patriotism") as fostering chauvinistic intolerance for minorities.[28] Unlike the thinkers of the Romantic Epoch, with whom he otherwise shared many ideas and illusions, he was aware of the growth of national aspirations among the non-Polish peoples of the former Commonwealth, but hoped that memories of common history would prevail and that all problems could be solved on the basis of democratic freedom and regional autonomy. Hence, he imagined the restored Polish state as a Switzerland of Eastern Europe.[29]

Thus, in the second half of the 1880s, Polish patriots had to choose between two radically different conceptions of the "Polish nation": the old, historical conception of a multiethnic political nation (represented by Limanowski) and the new, "peasantist" conception, narrowly ethnic and pretending to have had nothing in common with historical "Polishness." This situation did not last long. The concept of nation evolved in the direction of overcoming the sharp contrast between the ethno-linguistic nation of the peasantry and the "historical" nation of the gentry.

An instructive illustration of this process was Popławski's evolution from populism to nationalism—an evolution which made him one of the founders of the National Democratic Party (the *Endeks*). As a nationalist,

Popławski defined the modern Polish nation in ethno-linguistic terms while trying to preserve as much as possible from the heritage of the "historical" nation. This led him to stress that national character is also a product of common history and that renouncing historical heritage would amount to a de-politicization of the "ethnographic nation," thus making it politically innocent and palatable even to Muscovite patriots.[30] In contrast to Wysłouch, he was therefore adamant in defending the interests of the Polish minorities of the eastern Borderlands, especially in eastern Galicia where the position of the Poles was threatened by the Ukrainian national movement. He contemptuously rejected the "humanitarian" interpretation of national rights, claiming that national individuality and national interests often demand expansion beyond strictly ethnographic territory. Sometimes he justified such demands by invoking old romantic notions of "ages of common history" or "common spiritual culture."[31] On the whole, however, the emphasis on language, ethnicity, and culture was much more characteristic of his nationalism than the appeal to historic rights. Like Wysłouch, he wanted to contribute to the national awakening among the Polish-speaking population of upper Silesia, Mazuria, and other territories which had not belonged to the Polish state for centuries. He did not condemn the Jagellonian traditions, but thought that in the present situation the Poles should return rather to the tradition of their medieval Piast monarchy and concentrate above all on the German danger. He accused Polish politicians of stubbornly cherishing dreams of Vilnius (Wilno) and Kiev while, at the same time, neglecting Poznań, almost forgetting about Gdańsk and completely forgetting about Królewiec (Königsberg).[32] His claim to the Piast heritage was based not only on ethno-linguistic grounds but on geopolitical considerations as well. He feared that without Poznania, Silesia, access to the Baltic Sea and the whole of the Eastern Prussia, a future Poland would be too weak to exist as a truly independent state.[33]

As to the Easter frontiers of the future Poland, Popławski rejected both the "ethnographical principle" and the romantic dream of the restoration of the ancient, multiethnic, and multilingual Commonwealth. He wanted to incorporate only those parts of the Ukrainian, Belarusian, and Lithuanian territories in which the Poles were, in his estimation, strong enough to dominate the non-Polish population and subject it to a gradual Polonization. His ideal was a nationally homogeneous state. A Polish national community composed of many different ethnic and linguistic groups was in his view a relic of feudalism, incompatible with modern nationalism and the realities of the modern world.

Whether we like it or not, there was much truth in this view. This is not an evaluative judgment: modernity has long ceased to be regarded as a synonym of something unequivocally good and commendable. But our increased ambivalence about modernity does not change the well-established fact that modern nations are products of modernization and that modern nationalism is (to quote Gellner once more) a species of patriotism favoring cultural homogeneity—a homogeneity "based on a culture striving to be a high (literate) culture."[34] This was exactly Popławski's case.

Modern nations presuppose the effective "nationalization" of the masses. In Central and Eastern Europe this meant, on the one hand, raising the masses from raw "ethnic material" to a national consciousness, based upon high (literate) culture, and, on the other hand, dividing the population of the existing states along ethno-linguistic lines. This was bound to destroy not only the actual existing multinational empires (the Austro-Hungarian and the Russian), but also the ideal of the "non-modernized" Polish patriots of the Romantic Epoch: the ideal of the restoration of Poland as a multiethnic political nation within the frontiers of the Old Jagellonian Commonwealth. We can question the outcome of this process of modern nationbuilding: after all, the intensity of ethnic conflicts in the region dangerously increased, leading often to terrible human tragedies. But who said that modernization could be achieved without such tragedies? The general problem of the price of modernization is, certainly, of crucial importance, but we cannot discuss it here. Our task is much more limited. Since we are dealing with the relationship between modernization and national consciousness in Poland, we have to answer a concrete question: whose nationalism was more modern, Limanowski's, or Popławski's? Whose conceptions were more in tune with the process of forming modern nations in the East-Central Europe?

Irrespective of our personal sympathies, we have to say that at the end of the nineteenth century the most modern, and actively modernizing, form of Polish nationalism was represented by Popławski. But precisely because of this Limanowski's ideas might prove to be more relevant for the post-modern and post-nationalist epoch.

References

1.   See Andrzej Walicki, *Philosophy and Romantic Nationalism: The Case of Poland* (Oxford, 1982), pp. 59–93.
2.   See ibid., pp. 229–36.
3.   Adam Krzysztopór (Tomasz Potocki), *O urządzeniu stosunków rolniczych w Polsce* (Poznań, 1851), pp. vii–viii.
4.   Józef Gołuchowski, *Rozbiór kwestii wlościanskiej w. Polsce i w Rosji w 1850 r.* (Poznań, 1851), pp. 47–48.
5.   Ibid., pp. 227–40.
6.   See Ryszarda Czepulis-Rastenis, *Myśl społeczna twórców Towarzystwa Rolniczego (1842–1861),* (Wrocław, 1964).

7.   Stefan Bobrowski. See Wilhelm Feldman, *Dzieje polskiej mysli politycznej w okresie porozbiorowym*, vol. 1, (Cracow [no date]), p. 396.

8.   See August Cieszkowski, "On the Co-ordination of Intellectual Aims and Works in the Grand Duchy of Posen," in Andre Liebich, ed., *Selected Writings of August Cieszkowski*, (Cambridge, 1979), pp. 98–101. Cf. Andrzej Walicki, *Philosophy and Romantic Nationalism*, part II, ch. III and V.

9.   See Andrzej Jaszczuk, *Spór pozytywistów z konserwatystami o przyszłość Polski 1870–1903* (Warsaw, 1986), pp. 151–55 and 163.

10.   Ibid., p. 148.

11.   See ibid., ch. II and IV.

12.   Ibid., pp. 219–20.

13.   See Alina Molska, Introduction to the anthology *Pierwsze pokolenie marksistów polskich*, 2 vols., ed., Alina Molska (Warsaw, 1962).

14.   See Alina Molska, ed., *Pierwsze pokolenie marksistów polskich*, vol. 2, pp. 119 and 496.

15.   A sympathetic analysis of their views has been provided by Marcin Król in his book *Konserwatyści a niepodległość: Studia nad polską myślą konserwatywną XIX wieku* (Warsaw, 1985), ch. V–VI. For a selection of the Stańczyks' writings see Marcin Król, ed., *Stańczycy. Antologia myśli spotecznej i politycznej konserwatystów krakówskich* (Warsaw, 1985).

16.   Józef Szujski, *O falszywej historii jako mistrzyni falszywej polityki. Rozprawy i artykuły* (Warsaw, 1991), p. 237.

17.   Stefan Buszczyński, *Obrona spotwarzonego narodu* (Cracow, 1888), vol. 2, pp. 233–39. As we can see, Buszczyński saw the West as predatory, worshipping brutal power and, therefore, embodying "tough" values; in contrast to this, he associated Poland with "soft" values, such as peacefulness, consent, democratic mildness, defense of human rights at the expense of state power, and so forth. This was typical of Polish thought, both in the case of thinkers who glorified Polish national character and in the case of those who (like Brzozowski or Dmowski) wanted to change it. In other countries of East-Central Europe this syndrome was reversed: "the rebellion against Western values" was directed against liberal humanitarianism, democracy based on human rights, etc. See Ivan T. Berend, *The Crisis Zone of Europe: An Interpretation of East-Central European History in the First Half of the Twentieth Century*, trans. Adrienne Makkay-Chambers (Cambridge, 1986), pp. 30–31.

18.   Ibid., p. 239.

19.   Stanisław Szczepanowski, *Nędza Galicji w cyfrach i program energicznego rozwoju*, 2nd ed. (L'viv, 1888), p. 49.

20.   Ibid., p. 100.

21.   Ibid., p. 22.

22.   See Stanisław Szczepanowski, *Idea polska. Wybór pism*, ed., Stanisław Borzym (Warsaw, 1988).

23.   See Magdalena Opalski and Israel Bartal, *Poles and Jews: A Failed Brotherhood* (Hanover and London, 1992), pp. 44–47.

24.   Ibid., pp. 51–53.

25.   These expectations were based upon the durable phenomenon of the so-called two-level national consciousness among the Polish (or Polonized) gentry of the former Grand Duchy of Lithuania. It consisted in seeing oneself as belonging to two national communities at the same time: the broader one (Polish) and the narrower

one (Lithuanian), both of them conceived in historico-political terms, not ethnically. See Juliusz Bardach, "O świadomości narodowej Polaków na Litwie i Bialorusi," in Wojciech Wrzesiński, ed., *Między Polską etniczną a historyczną* (Wrocław, 1988), p. 232.

26. See Jan Ludwik Popławski, *Pisma polityczne* (Cracow-Warsaw, 1910), vol. 1, pp. 134–46.

27. According to Peter Brock, this series of articles was written by Adam Zakrzewski, but reflected the standpoint of the editor of *The Social Review*, Bolesław Wysłouch. (See Peter Brock, *Nationalism and Populism in Partitioned Poland: Selected Essays* (London, 1973), pp. 181–211). Other authors attribute the authorship directly to Wysłouch. (See Andrzej Kudlaszyk, *Myśl społeczno-polityczna Bolesława Wysłoucha* [Warsaw-Wroclaw, 1978], pp. 96–103).

28. See Kazimiera Janina Cottam, *Bolesław Limanowski (1835–1935): A Study in Nationalism and Socialism* (Boulder, Colorado, 1978), pp. 91–92.

29. Bolesław Limanowski, *Naród i państwo* (Cracow, 1906), p. 99.

30. Popławski, *Pisma polityczne*, vol. 1, p. 195.

31. Ibid., pp.110–111.

32. Ibid., vol. 2, p. 15.

33. Ibid., p. 393.

34. Ernest Gellner, *Nations and Nationalism* (Ithaca, 1983), p. 138.

LECTURE III

The Period of Cultural Modernism and Political Activism, 1895–1914

The Double Revolt against Positivism

The new period in Polish intellectual history began, approximately, in the middle of the 1890s. It was characterized by a double revolt—both cultural and political—against Positivism. In the first sense, it was a revolt against Positivistic scientism, empiricism, evolutionary naturalism, and utilitarianism, in the name of spirituality, free creativity, rehabilitation of the irrational forces of the human psyche, and a metaphysical search for the Absolute. In the second sense it was a revolt against Positivism in the specifically Polish meaning of this term, that is, against the program of apolitical organic work, aimed at furthering the cultural and economic progress of the nation. The first revolt reflected a general shift in European culture, known as the birth of cultural "Modernism," or (to use H. Stuart Hughes' terminology) as the beginning of an anti-naturalistic "reorientation of European social thought."[1] The second revolt was a response to events in Poland, namely, to the marked activization and politicization of the masses which found expression in patriotic demonstrations (like the mass demonstration in Warsaw on 17 April 1894, celebrating the centenary of Jan Kiliński's insurrection), or in the spontaneous self-organization and the impressive strike actions of the industrial workers (like the nine-day, bloodily suppressed strike of sixty thousand Polish textile workers in Łódź who, in May 1892, revolted against the ethnic segregation of job categories in factories).[2] It was also a result of the fact that the fear of direct political activity, which had characterized the generation whose formative life experience was the defeat of the insurrection of 1863 and its disastrous consequences, was now being overcome. The younger generation was impatient with the political passivity of the Positivist intelligentsia, and wanted to engage in an "active politics," guided by political parties. At the beginning of the period under discussion three such parties emerged: the party of the so-called National Democrats (*Endeks*), formally organized in 1893 under the name "National League," and two socialist parties—the Polish Socialist Party (PPS, founded in 1892) and the Social Democracy of the Kingdom of Poland (SDKP, founded in 1893 and transformed in 1900 into SDKPiL—the Social Democratic Party of the Kingdom of Poland and

Lithuania). All of these parties proved to be more influential and viable than other political groupings, and can thus legitimately be treated as the most important political forces of the Polish society of the period.

The National Democrats, a radically nationalistic and increasingly anti-semitic party, tried to combine militant activism with programmatic realism, cautiously testing the limits of the possible. Their idea of "active policy" was conceived as a third way between the conciliation with the status quo and suicidal "political romanticism." In other words, it was an attempt to go beyond apolitical "organic work," while, at the same time, stopping short of a national insurrection. The National Democrats brought organized pressure on the Russian authorities to force them to make further and further concessions. At the same time they put concerted moral pressure on their compatriots by boycotting collaborators, urging people to sign various collective petitions to the government, and, above all, by creating a sense of national solidarity. They hoped that this would ensure for their party the position of moral arbiter in national affairs and force hesitant individuals to be obedient to its will. They also engaged in underground educative and publishing activities with the aim of awakening the masses and forming political elites among them. The activization of the masses thus achieved was to serve as the most powerful means of extracting concessions. Therefore, the "realism" of this program, which consisted of an emphatic rejection of romantic revolutionism, was very different from the "cabinet realism" of Wielopolski.[3] It was a program of organizing Polish society from below in order to make it self-conscious and capable of struggling for national ends. Small wonder that this aspect of the National Democrats' historical record proved appealing to the Polish democratic opposition of the 1970s, otherwise so different from the *Endeks'* political mentality.[4]

The PPS was a party composed of both Marxist and non-Marxist socialists who saw the industrial proletariat as the strongest and most progressive class of Polish society, and who wanted to combine serving its class interests with the struggle for an independent Poland. Its ideology was somewhat eclectic and ill-defeated, but because of this, it could appeal to an astonishing variety of people. They ranged from convinced socialists—as different as Bolesław Limanowski, deeply steeped in the Polish romantic tradition, and Kazimierz Kelles-Krauz, a principled, though non-dogmatic Marxist—to patriots whose main concern was winning the working class for the national cause. The tension between the socialist and nationalist tendencies within the PPS caused it to split in 1906 into the PPS-Left, which in 1918 joined the newly-emerged Communist Party of Poland, and the PPS-Revolutionary Faction, headed by Józef Piłsudski, who devoted all of his energy to the struggle for independence and who, after achieving this end, quickly distanced himself from socialism.

The SDKP, whose chief theorist was Rosa Luxemburg, has been described as "the first independent party of the communist type, which inasmuch as it emphasized the purely proletarian character of the socialist movement, refused to have anything to do with Polish (or any other) nationalism, and professed absolute fidelity to Marxian doctrine."[5] Its program was based on the assumption that the Polish lands, due to "an entirely objective historical process, independent of anyone's will,"[6] were "organically incorporated" into the three partitioning powers. It defined itself not as a Polish party, but as a territorial party representing the multiethnic working class of the Congress Kingdom and historical Lithuania; a party seeing itself as a part of an all-Russian workers' movement and aiming at a revolutionary transformation of the Russian Empire within its existing frontiers. As such, it was deeply committed to combatting all national separatisms, as dividing the workers and contradicting the centralizing tendency of progress. Hence, its members did not take part in the debate over modernization in all parts of partitioned Poland, let alone over national self-definition. For that reason the SDKP is much less relevant for our topic than the PPS and the *Endeks*.

The cultural revolt against Positivism, best represented by the literary movement known as Young Poland, brought about a spectacular revival of romantic interpretations of Polish national character and Polish history. The romantic idea of nations as separate embodiments of spirit was revived on the pages of the L'viv journal *Odrodzenie* (*Regeneration*, published in 1903–1906), whose editors saw Szczepanowski as their spiritual leader. The metaphysical philosopher, Wincenty Lutosławski, world-famous as an expert on Plato, worked out a system of evolutionary spiritualist monadology, based upon the romantic idea of progressive reincarnation (which he found in the writings of Polish messianic poets, Adam Mickiewicz and Juliusz Słowacki). The Polish nation was presented in this system as a community of the most developed and hence most perfect spirits, leading humankind towards its final destiny: universal regeneration and salvation on earth, the prefiguration of which could be seen in the ancient Polish-Lithuanian Commonwealth. Another neo-romantic, Artur Górski, elaborated a philosophy of Polish history which showed the Poles as a tragic nation, martyrs of freedom. In his view, Poland had tried to realize a higher ideal than merely a well-organized state and for that reason was bound to fall a victim to its less morally demanding but better organized neighbors. (Better organized, the author explained, because it was much easier to organize national life on the basis of lower instincts than on higher moral aspirations).[7] In a more restrained form similar ideas were expressed by a historical publicist, Antoni Chołoniewski, whose *Spirit of Polish History* (*Duch dziejów Polski;* 1917) was a violent attack on the Cracow school in historiography, as denigrating the Polish past and espousing instead the Western materialism and cult of brute force.[8]

As we can see, romantic anti-Westernism proved able to appear once more in Polish intellectual life. But the neo-romantics of the Modernist Epoch were, from the point of view of our topic, much less important that the thinkers of the Romantic Epoch. The ideas of Joachim Lelewel and Mickiewicz, Edward Dembowski and Karol Libelt expressed the aspirations of the Polish national-liberation movement, while the views of Lutosławski, or Górski, represented only an elitist fashion, relevant, to some extent, for the understanding of the alienated modernist intellectuals but of no real significance for the processes of nationbuilding and national modernization in Poland.

In what follows, I shall concentrate, therefore, on the two currents of thought which were most effective in shaping the Polish mind on the eve of the independence: patriotic socialism, represented mostly (though not exclusively) by the PPS, and the integral nationalism of the National Democratic Party.

Patriotic Socialism

My presentation of patriotic socialism or, more broadly, working class national patriotism, will be limited to its three most representative and influential thinkers: Kazimierz Kelles-Krauz, the leading Marxist theorist of the PPS, Stanisław Brzozowski, the most influential literary critic and philosopher of culture of the period, and Edward Abramowski, a co-founder of the PPS who developed an original anarcho-syndicalist theory of "stateless socialism."

Kelles-Krauz developed his views in a constant polemic with Rosa Luxemburg.[9] He agreed with her that the Congress Kingdom had become the most industrialized part of the Russian Empire but drew from this completely different conclusions. Lack of national independence, he held, did not promote industrial development in the Congress Kingdom. On the contrary: this situation chained it to a backward, semi-Asiatic Russia, whose autocratic government could reintroduce tariff barriers at will if it happened to serve the interests of Russian industrialists. The Polish bourgeoisie, especially the bourgeoisie of non-Polish background, shunned the idea of national independence because of their notorious cowardice, not due to any sound economic considerations. But even if it were otherwise, there was no reason to identify national interest, especially proletarian interest, with the transient commercial needs of the bourgeoisie. Neither was it possible to share Luxemburg's view that the proletariat was not interested in creating new class stated. Such a view, Kelles-Krauz argued, was a dangerous relic of Bakuninism in the workers' movement.

In his own approach to the "Polish question" Kelles-Krauz relied on the old diagnosis of Marx and Engels: he saw Russia as the cornerstone of European reaction, and Poland as an eastern outpost of the progressive West. He also cherished the illusion that the Lithuanian, Ukrainian, and Belarusian populations of the ancient Polish-Lithuanian Commonwealth were still "gravitating" towards Poland.[10] He thought that Belarus, Lithuania, and his native Latvia would be satisfied with national autonomy within the restored Polish state, while Ukraine would choose a kind of loose federation with Poland. Such a solution, he argued, would be much better for these young nations than remaining within the boundaries of an essentially "Asiatic" Russia. He even claimed that reestablishing their links with Poland would be a step toward independence for which, he thought, they were not then ready.

Despite these political anachronisms in his thinking, Kelles-Krauz drew from Marxism important arguments for the view that Poland should be modernized on the Western model—through national liberation and political democracy. The only difference from the Western model was to be a much greater role for the working class, as the social force representing the modernized sector of Polish economy, vitally interested in both further economic modernization and national freedom.

Kelles-Krauz's support of Marx's and Engels' view on the peculiar importance of the Polish question did not prevent him from recognizing that, in principle, the so-called "new nations" had an equally valid right to national independence. Following Karl Kautsky (and here abandoning Marx and Engels), he strongly emphasized the nationbuilding role of a common language. The importance of the linguistic bond, he asserted, increased with horizontal and vertical social mobility, characteristic of capitalist development. The ability to communicate in the same language now became a particularly strong social tie in a universal breakdown of those traditional social structures in which the need for communication between different social strata had been much less. As a result, the boundaries of common-language territories delivered national markets, and so modern nationalities came into being.

Luxemburg's argument that pan-national interests are pure fiction since a real existence (apart from culture) can be attributed only to antagonistic class interests was seen by Kelles-Krauz as an utter vulgarization of Marxism. It was absurd, he maintained, to put class interests above national interests because the viewpoint of each class and, especially, the proletarian viewpoint was merely a certain interpretation of the interests of a given nation as a whole. In contrast to castes and estates, modern classes are not separate from each other and alien to each other. They oppose each other within a certain national unity; they differ profoundly in their understanding of the common good, but, if mature enough, they cannot indulge in particularist class egoism.[11] Political democracy—a necessary condition for modern civilized forms of class struggle—can take deep root only in a state whose citizens are not committed to irredentism, or to the oppression of national minorities. Therefore, an independent national state is necessary for both the national bourgeoisie and the working class. The latter needs it even more than the former because the proletarian class interest demands *full* political democratization, and cannot be satisfied with half-measures.

The obvious conclusion from this argument was that the Polish working class was the best exponent of the Polish national interest, progressively conceived; in other words, that Polish workers had become a "national class" in Marx's and Engels' understanding of this term. It was they, not the bourgeoisie, who were to play the hegemonic role in both national liberation and the bourgeois-democratic transformation of Poland.

Thanks to Brzozowski, a similar view of the national mission of the workers became translated into a language which appealed to wide strata of non-party intellectuals concerned with problems of national regeneration and cultural crisis.[12] He initially was strongly influenced by the image of the intelligentsia as an elite of knowledge and heroic sacrifice, committed to disinterested social service and, therefore, being the natural leader of the nation. His Marxist-inspired "philosophy of work," however, led him to the conclusions that the intelligentsia was a product of a double alienation: alienation from the productive process, which deprived it of a "foundation in being," and social alienation, due to its "liberation" from all forms of social discipline, which made it helplessly uprooted. In contrast to this, in Brzozowski's eyes the working class was a true vanguard of humanity, its "foundation in being," a social class with the deepest roots in history. It compressed within itself, as it were, the entire history of human labor, and, at the same time, was endowed with the great universal mission of carrying through a double liberation: the Promethean conquest of nature through industrial modernization, and, at a later stage, the social liberation of labor. The latter was to be achieved by attaining a level of self-discipline which would safeguard high productivity without any need for external compulsion. As such, the working class represented the strongest and the healthiest type of life; the intelligentsia should become the consciousness of this life-type, giving up all dreams of an independent mission, let alone unhealthy strivings for national leadership.

This general view of the intelligentsia became even more severe when applied to the situation in Poland. The Polish intelligentsia, Brzozowski thought, had failed everywhere. The events of the revolution of 1905–1907 proved its failure as a patriotic force, while showing at the same time that the Polish workers were the only force capable of struggling for national and social liberation. The intelligentsia failed disastrously as a modernizing force because its cultural production—works of arts, ideas—was hopelessly immature, lagging behind the level of modernity achieved by the industry of the more developed parts of Poland, and contrasting sharply with the conscious energy, maturity, and modernity of the Polish workers. The conservative part of the intelligentsia reproduced in its thinking the infantilized mentality of the effeminated and senile Polish gentry, whose "ideogenetic type" was the traditionalist Catholic family, living parasitically in a white-painted manor house, without thinking and worrying, cultivating its patriotic memories and confidently believing that Almighty God will reward the Poles for their childish innocence.[13] The progressive part tried to draw from the various traditions of the romantic struggles for independence, without being able to combine noble romantic idealism with a "tough historical realism," without any attempt to modernize the historical consciousness of the Poles. Because of this, the spiritual richness of the Polish romantic tradition was not transformed into a source of national energy. On the contrary, loyalty to these values became transformed into a passive cult of national martyrdom and a morbid idealization of defeat.[14]

All of these arguments supported Brzozowski's conviction that the Polish cause rested on the strength and cultural maturity of the Polish workers. Polish industrial workers were, in his view, the most advanced, most modern part of Polish society, representing the long-ranging interests of the entire nation and able therefore to exercise a "moral dictatorship" in national life. Polish workers were entitled to this for two reasons: their work, which was raising Poland to the level of civilizational modernity, and their class struggle, which was paving the way for national independence. National feeling among the workers was, in Brzozowski's view, an unquestionable reality. Indeed, it could not have been otherwise: every human being, upon reaching a certain stage of development, experiences nationhood as the "deepest reality," the "organ of self-knowledge" and the "foundation in being."

In 1906 Brzozowski saw himself as an unorthodox Marxist and a supporter of the PPS. In the next few years, however, he moved away from Marxism, and became bitterly critical of socialism as a political movement. His ardent belief in the regenerative mission of the working class remained unchanged, but "political socialism" became in his eyes a parasitic movement—a movement of the "economically incompetent intelligentsia," sponging on the workers' movement and trying to use it for its own ends. An important personal reason for his disillusionment with all socialist parties was their unproven accusation that he was an agent of the Tsarist Okhrana (secret police). After this painful experience Brzozowski turned his back on "party socialism" and embraced instead the syndicalist conception of the workers' movement represented by Georges Sorel. As a result, he became critical of Marxism and elaborated a new version of his "philosophy of work," emphasizing the ontological status of nationality and the positive, disciplining function of custom and tradition.

Brzozowski's distrust of "political socialism" and of the intellectuals offering their services as leaders of the workers' movement, was fully shared by Edward Abramowski.[15] But Abramowski's interpretation of syndicalism and his view of the regenerative mission of the workers were diametrically opposed to Brzozowski's ideas. To put it briefly, Abramowski proclaimed liberation *from labor*, while Brzozowski stood for liberation *through labor*. The former praised laziness and unconstrained spontaneity, while the latter identified freedom with disciplined autocreation. The highest values for Abramowski were evangelical brotherhood, universal friendship, and the disinterested contemplation of beauty; Brzozowski saw these as "soft" values, and set against them the "hard" ones—Promethean struggle, a severe work ethic, and the Nietzschean "will of power." Both thinkers criticized intellectualism and scientism, but from the different angles: Brzozowski stressed the priority of the productive praxis of a historically developing collective subject, while Abramowski wanted to get rid of instrumental "practicality." He wanted to awaken the non-reified "deeper self" of human beings, and thus liberate them from the narrow cage of *principio individuationis*. Using modern terminology, we can legitimately say that Brzozowski preached radical modernization and powerfully expressed the so-called "labor paradigm" of the philosophy of the subject.[16] Abramowski, on the other hand, can be seen as a consistent critic of modernity, one of the first "post-modern" thinkers of our century.

All these differences between the two thinkers were reflected in their concepts of nation and attitudes toward Westernism. Abramowski's vision of the Polish nation was Eastern-oriented, nostalgic, refusing to accept the idea of linguistic and cultural homogeneity. Born in Ukraine, he remembered his birthplace as a wonderful world of multiethnic and multicultural harmony, an embodiment of the noble spirit of the Commonwealth. In a programmatic article published on the eve of World War I he adamantly rejected the idea of an "ethnographic Poland," calling it "an idea born of fear and brought up by impotence and despair." Fatherland, he argued, has nothing in common with an ethno-linguistic community: "The fatherland is created by evolutionary means: by the history of peoples living together on the same land, and by constant intermingling of blood and spirit . . . And it is for this reason that peoples and tribes which, even if they speak different languages, have constantly intermingled through the ages and generations, always have one fatherland, and this fatherland is for them not something external, artificial and imposed, but, on the contrary, constitutes their own soul."[17] This meant that all peoples of the Old Commonwealth continued to share a common and indivisible fatherland. In another article of 1914 Abramowski went even further, stating confidently that Ukrainians and Lithuanians were simply parts of the Polish nation. He wrote: "The Polish nation has always been composed of these three peoples: Polish, Lithuanian, and Ukrainian. And what God himself has united, nobody can disunite."[18]

From Brzozowski's point of view this was an anachronistic idea, wishful thinking, and an idealistic escape from reality. He himself knew Ukraine very well and did not see it as an idyllic place. He was fully aware of the depth of its ethnic conflicts: the Polish landowners in the Ukrainian lands were in his view the most backward and narrow-minded part of the Polish nobility, completely untouched by nineteenth-century progress. He did not pay special attention to ethnicity but, nevertheless, defined nations in cultural terms, not as historico-territorial units; hence he could not claim that Ukrainians and Poles belonged to the same nation. And, unlike Abramowski, he was always bitterly critical of nostalgic idealizations of Polish life in the so-called "Eastern Borderlands." He wanted Poland to be a distinctively Western nation, modernized on the Western model, espousing the Promethean and Faustian values of Western civilization.

Integral Nationalism

The main ideologist of the National Democrats, Roman Dmowski, developed Popławski's ideas in the direction of a consistent "integral nationalism." Under the Polish conditions, however, integral nationalism had to contain a severe critique of the national past and a program of a radical modernization of the national character. This emphasis is conspicuously visible in Dmowski's programmatic book *Thoughts of the Modern Pole* (*Myśli nowoczesnego Polaka;* 1902).

The modern Pole, Dmowski claimed, should not be merely a "patriot," a man attached to the fatherland as a certain collection of civil rights and liberties. Rather, he should be a self-conscious "nationalist," a member of a nation as a living organism which has its unique cultural individuality and which demands of individuals a total devotion to its collective interest.[19] In contrast to "half-Poles" who try to deal with national conflicts from the point of view of objective justice, the modern Pole knows that neutrality is a fiction, a mask of moral weakness. He therefore does not try to conceal, let alone weaken, his unequivocal commitment to the cause of his own nation. He realizes that moral criteria, as such, should be applied only in the sphere of private life, but not in the sphere of conflicts between nations. True, Dmowski continues, politics should not be simply immoral, but morality in politics consists precisely in taking responsibility for one's own nation (hence the requirement to avoid irresponsible actions), and in the understanding that political interests of other nations, even if they collide with one's own, are perfectly legitimate (hence the postulate to treat the enemy respectfully, to understand his motives and to avoid reacting to his action with blind hatred). But this should not be confused with subordinating national interests to supranational justice and other romantic fictions. Modern nationalists should be clearly aware that "the only principle in international relations is that of strength or weakness, never that of being morally right or wrong."[20]

From this point of view the entire tradition of Polish romantic nationalism, with its ideal of brotherhood of nations and ethicization of politics, appeared to be a testimony of naïve idealism and political immaturity. The idea of Polish "moral superiority" was seen by Dmowski as an idealization of weakness; attributing to the Poles a sacred mission to fight for the salvation of other nations was for him morally repellent.

Dmowski's criticism of romantic nationalism did not spare the national insurrections of the Romantic Epoch, so dear to the hearts of both old-fashioned patriots and the patriotic socialists of the PPS. He had the civil courage to state that the entire tradition of nineteenth-century uprisings was a tradition of humiliating defeats, unworthy of being celebrated by "modern Poles." Even more negative was his view of the revolution of 1905–1907. He saw it as having played into the hands of Germans, because the level of anarchy and the destruction of industry in the Congress Kingdom opened the Russian markets to the enterprising industrialists of Germany.[21]

As is well known, Dmowski was the main representative of a "pro-Russian" orientation in Polish politics. His book *Germany, Russia and the Polish Question* (*Niemcy, Rosja i kwestia polska;* 1908) presented Polish interests, and the very survival of Poland, as threatened mostly by Germany; he, therefore, demanded a policy aimed at an understanding with Russia. Due to this he was able to perform an important political role during World War I—he was recognized as representing those Poles who had sided with the Entente and thus had the honor of signing the treaty of Versailles in the name of the restored Poland. It should be stressed, however, that his "pro-Russian" orientation was not bound up with "Slavophilism" as a cultural option. On the contrary: in his views on the Polish past and future Dmowski was a cultural Westernizer. His favorite hero in Polish history was King Boleslaus the Brave (992–1025), whom he credited with formulating the fundamental principles of Polish politics that were equally valid in the eleventh and in the twentieth century, principles such as strong statehood, Western civilization, a constant alertness to the German threat. He regretted that the union with Lithuania channeled Polish energy to the steppes of the East, at the cost of neglecting Polish interests in the West, especially access to the Baltic Sea. He agreed with those Polish historians who saw the gentry democracy as a deplorable deviation from the Western model of national development. Accordingly, he praised the eighteenth-century reformers, creators of the May 3rd Constitution, as ones who returned to this model and rejected the "monstrous political liberalism" of the Sarmatian Commonwealth.[22] Equally occidentalist were his views on Russia. He emphasized the oriental elements in the Russian autocracy, the long tradition of disrespect—if not outright contempt—for the law, and the inconsistencies and failures of Russia's Westernization. These failures manifested themselves, above all, in the weakness of a civil society dominated by different oppositional and revolutionary groups, but lacking strong, autonomous social forces. He was thus "pro-Russian" not because of any disinterested cultural sympathy, but as a consequence of his analysis of Polish national interest in the given geopolitical situation. This analysis convinced him that Poland as an independent state is conceivable only as an ally of Russia—if only because it cannot exist as an ally of Germany, let alone in conditions of a Russo-German alliance. He clung to this conclusion even after the Bolshevik revolution. He wrote: "The Soviet rule in Russia will come to an end, but Russia will remain, and our relationship with what is permanent in it—the Russian nation—is more important than transient governments."[23]

To be sure, Dmowski's program for the modernization of Poland was not confined to the task of national reeducation, in the sense of creating a new model of national *consciousness*. It was also a program of elaborating a model of modern nationhood, and of securing for the Polish nation an optimal territorial shape.

In Dmowski's view the notion of a multilingual and multiethnic nation made sense in the case of the old "nation of the gentry," but not in that of a democratized nation, composed of all strata of the population. Modern nations are social entities cemented by linguistic, cultural and, consequently, ethnic unity (although most of them had been originally composed of different ethnic elements). Unity based upon homogeneity is thus an essential feature of modern nationhood. But the ways of achieving national unity might be different; this accounts for the continuing existence of different types of nations. Dmowski distinguished two such types: the "State-nationality" and the "linguistic or ethnographical nationality."[24] The first, he argued, is dominant in the West, because in Western Europe the boundaries among the separate States were relatively stable, and their inhabitants—although originally different in race and speaking different languages—had lived through a series of generations as members of one state, under common institutions. The second type is dominant in Central and Eastern Europe, because there the frontiers of the states were unstable, and, as a result, the strongest factor in the formation of nationality was the community of language.

The strong point in this view was the realistic recognition of the legitimacy of the so-called "new nations" of East-Central Europe—nations lacking a

continuous tradition of statehood, and, therefore, formed "from below," in
the process of "national self-awakening" on the ethno-linguistic basis. This,
however, did not entail automatic recognition of their rights to national
independence, since some of them might never be capable of creating and
maintaining an independent national state. In Dmowski's view this was the
case of Lithuanians, as a nation too small (he thought) to develop separately
from Poland. More complex was Dmowski's attitude to the Ukrainian
question. He envisaged three possibilities. If the Ukrainians, or at least part
of them, could be Polonized, then they should be Polonized as quickly and
as radically as possible. If they had a strong potential to develop as a
separate Ruthenian nation, then a tough confrontation with militant Polish
nationalism would help them to acquire a well-defined national identity and
necessary political experience. The third possibility, the worst one for the
Poles, would be the replacement of Polish influence in Ukraine by a
successful Russification of its population.[25]

At any rate, Dmowski was not prepared to reduce Polish territorial
demands to the ethno-linguistic boundaries. True, he especially emphasized
the need to regain the ethnically Polish parts of Silesia or Pomerania, but he
never accepted the idea of losing L'viv or Vilnius. In order to justify this
position he introduced a new typological division: a division into "small"
and "great" nations. Despite all their national faults, Poles were, in his view,
a "great" nation—that is, one whose cultural influence and legitimate
interests transcended its ethnographical boundaries. The "National Territory"
of such a nation, he reasoned, cannot be reduced to its "ethnic territory"; it
must include all lands where its political and cultural influence is dominant.[26]
According to this logic, Poles should definitely abandon the romantic
dream of restoring their state within the frontiers of 1772, but, at the same
time, fight to the bitter end for their ascendancy in the Vilnius region and in
the Western parts of Belarus and Ukraine.

Dmowski's understanding of the consequences of such a solution was
obviously not farsighted enough. He grossly underestimated Lithuanian
nationalism. He did not fully realize how dangerous and counterproductive
his program of Polonizing the Eastern Galicia was. Even worse were the
consequences of his belief that Poles should rid themselves of moral
scruples, and pursue their political and economic interests with the same
brutality which characterized the actions of the German Hakatists in the
Prussian part of Poland. These ideological prescriptions and the actions they
inspired added fuel to the conflicts with national minorities, and made these
conflicts virtually unsolvable. Especially harmful were Dmowski's views on
the Jewish question—both for the Jews and for the Poles. His evolution in this
question, leading from a relatively moderate economic and political anti-
semitism to a violent racial anti-semitism[27], was harmful also for his own
political credo: it undermined the programmatic anti-emotionalism of the

credo, made its followers obsessed with looking everywhere for "Jewish plots" and, in the 1930s, pushed most of them into semi-fascist positions.

One of the unintended consequences of Dmowski's nationalism was, paradoxically, a drastic weakening of the Polish influence in the "Eastern Borderlands" of the former Commonwealth. This influence was alive and strong because the Polish landed gentry of these lands was not entirely isolated; because Polishness remained attractive to a vast category of people whose national consciousness was complex, and multilayered, who combined in themselves different loyalties and balanced them against each other. But Dmowski's program of nationalist modernization aimed at eradicating such multiple loyalties, as being incompatible with well-defined modern nations. Dmowski failed to predict that forcing the principle of a single, undivided national loyalty would promote the cause of the non-Polish nationalisms of the region.

References

1.   See Henry Stuart Hughes, *Consciousness and Society. The Reorientation of European Social Thought 1890–1930* (New York, 1958).
2.   See Adam Próchnik, *Bunt łódzki w roku 1892. Studjum historyczne* (Warsaw, 1932).
3.   See Aleksander Hall, "Dwa realizmy," *Tygodnik Powszechny* 28 (14 July 1985).
4.   See Bohdan Cywiński, *Rodowody niepokornych* (Warsaw, 1971), pp. 325–52; Barbara Toruńczyk (ed.) *Narodowa Demokracja. Antologia myśli politycznej "Przeglądu Wszechpolskiego"* (London, 1983); Adam Michnik, *Szanse polskiej demokracji* (London, 1984), pp. 214–41. In Michnik's view main merit of the program of the "National Democrats" was its tendency to reconstruct the "subjectivity" (*podmiotowość*) of society. (ibid., p. 231).
5.   Leszek Kolakowski, *Main Currents of Marxism: Its Origins, Growth and Dissolution* (Oxford, 1981), vol. 2, p. 17.
6.   Róża Luksemburg [Rosa Luxemburg], *Wybór pism* (Warsaw 1959), vol. 1, p. 60. For a comprehensive analysis of Luxemburg's views on the "national question" see Andrzej Walicki, "Rosa Luxemburg and the Question of Nationalism in Polish Marxism (1893–1914)," *The Slavonic and East European Review* 61, no. 4 (Oct. 1983).
7.   Artur Górski, *Ku czemu Polska szla?* (1915; quoted from the 3rd ed., Warsaw, 1921, p. 193).
8.   Antoni Chołoniewski, *Duch dziejów Polski* (Cracow, 1917).
9.   See Andrzej Walicki, "Rosa Luxemburg and the Question of Nationalism in Polish Marxism.(1893–1914)," *The Slavonic and East European Review* 61, no. 4 (Oct., 1983).
10.   Kazimierz Kelles-Krauz, *Pisma wybrane* (Warsaw, 1962) vol. 2, pp. 147–48.
11.   Ibid., p. 386.
12.   For a comprehensive monograph on Brzozowski see Andrzej Walicki, *Stanisław*

Brzozowski and the Polish Beginnings of "Western Marxism" (Oxford, 1989).

13. See Brzozowski's famous essay "Polska zdziecinniala" (*Infantilized Poland*) in his *Legenda Młodej Polski* (L'viv, 1910).

14. See Brzozowski, *Legenda Młodej Poski* (In Dziela wszystkie, t. VIII, Warsaw, 1937), p 377.

15. For a detailed comparative analysis of the views of these two thinkers see my article "Stanisław Brzozowski i Edward Abramowski," in Andrzej Walicki, *Polska, Rosja, marksizm. Studia z dziejów marksizmu i iego recepcji* (Warsaw, 1983), pp. 252–321.

It is no exaggeration to say that both thinkers provided a stock of ideas which exerted a profound influence on the Polish intelligentsia. The last revival of interest in Brzozowski's ideas took place in the 1970s—the period ofgreat illusions as to the possibility of rapid economic modernization in Poland. Brzozowski's ideas were attractive by then because they were seen as combining an intellectually exciting, unorthodox Marxism with a sort of working class nationalism, both culminating in a glorification of productive work (although in fact the work ethic in Poland was not offering any reasons for jubilation). The revival of Abramowski's ideas came soon afterwards, with the phenomenon of Solidarity. Polish intellectuals acting in its ranks became fascinated with Abramowski's vision of a self-governing society, which would ignore the agencies of the state and thereby regain its sovereign "subjectivity" (*podmiotowość*).

For these reasons Abramowski became the favorite thinker of Jan Józef Lipski, Jacek Kuroń and Adam Michnik, the most representative members of the Workers' Defence Committee (KOR). (See Michnik, *Szanse polskiej demokracji,* pp. 229–30 and 240–41). Wojciech Gielżyński wrote a book entitled "Edward Abramowski, a Harbinger of Solidarity" (*Edward Abramowski, zwiastun Solidarnośći* [London, 1986]). As a mass movement, however, Solidarity was not influenced by Abramowski's ideas.

16. Cf. Jürgen Habermas' critique of this paradigm in his *Theory of Communicative Action,* trans. Thomas McCarthy, 2 vols. (Boston, 1984–1987).

17. E. Abramowski, "Pomniejszyciele ojczyny," *Kurier Warszawski* 25–26 March, 1914. Quoted from E. Abramowski, *Pisma publicystyczne w sprawach robotniczych i chlopskich* (Warsaw, 1938), p. 272–73.

18. Ibid., p. 283.

19. Roman Dmowski, *Wybór pism* (New York 1988), vol. 1, pp. 26–8, 93.

20. Roman Dmowski, *Niemcy, Rosja i kwestia polska* (L'viv, 1908), pp. 235–6.

21. Roman Dmowski, *Polityka polska i odbudowanie państwa* (Warsaw, 1925), p. 61.

22. Roman Dmowski, *Wybór pism,* vol. 1, p. 104.

23. Roman Dmowski, *Polityka polska,* p. 501.

24. See Roman Dmowski, *The Problem of Central and Eastern Europe* (London, July 1917). This brochure published during World War I, was written with a special purpose: to explain to the leaders of the Entente the nationalities question in the East-Central Europe.

25. See Roman Dmowski, *Wybór pism,* vol. 1, pp. 67–68 (*Myśli nowoczesnego Polaka*).

In Dmowski's opinion, his position in this question should have been appreciated by Ukrainian nationalists as a sort of challenge. He understood that the concept of nation as a multiethnic, "spiritual community," combined with an idealization of the Old Commonwealth, could appeal only to people of Polish culture, especially "old-fashioned" patriots of the gentry and idealistic intellectuals. Ukrainian or Lithuanian nationalists had to perceive such ideas as an attempt to arrest the growth of modern national consciousness among their peoples.

26. Roman Dmowski, *Polityka polska*, pp. 103–10.

27. The main factor in this process was political activation of the Warsaw Jews, especially the Russian-speaking "Litvaks." The turning point was the year 1912, when a Jewish socialist became elected to the Russian Duma as a representative of Warsaw. See Andrzej Micewski, *Roman Dmowski* (Warsaw, 1971), pp. 190–94.

Concluding Remarks

The theme of my three lectures is too rich and vast to allow for straightforward conclusions. Therefore, I shall limit myself to formulating a few general observations which might be useful for discussing the problems involved in a comparative perspective.

First, Polish thought under the partitions shows that economic modernization is a part of modernization conceived more broadly—as a wholesale modernization of national life, from economy and society to national consciousness and culture. A similar case was presented by pre-revolutionary Russia: there, too, economic questions, especially the problem of the different ways of economic development, were seen as part of a larger national question, involving the problem of Russian self-definition, cultural identity, and so on. Russia, however, was not threatened as a nation; consequently in Russian thought, socioeconomic questions could occupy a central position without losing their relative autonomy, as was the case at the time of the classical controversy between the Russian populists and the Russian Marxists. In partitioned Poland the "national question," in its many dimensions, was so overwhelmingly important, and so central to intellectual life, that problems of economic development were, as a rule, totally subordinated to it.

Second, the problem of modernization, thus conceived, was bound up with the general civilizational option: pro-Western or anti-Western. For several reasons, however, many Poles tried to persuade themselves and others that such a question was absent from Polish intellectual history because, allegedly, for the Poles their sense of belonging to the West had always been something obvious and taken for granted. I have attempted to correct this wholly mistaken judgment by showing that "Westernism" began to prevail in partitioned Poland only in the "Positivist" period, that is, paradoxically, at the time of a temporary resignation to Poland's incorporation to Russia. In the Romantic Epoch, whose formative influence on national culture in Poland was probably the greatest, consistent "Westernizers" were a minority. The most characteristic thinkers of that time represented, as a rule, different variants of "anti-Westernism"—communitarian nationalism, agrarian socialism, Slavophile-colored messianism, and so forth. It is important to stress this fact because it opens up the possibility of seeing the ideological patterns in Poland in a comparative perspective—as peculiar to Poland, but, nevertheless, comparable to ideological options facing other countries of the region, including Germany and Russia.

The final victory of a definitely Westernizing orientation in Polish thought, reflecting the successes in the industrialization of the Congress

Kingdom, coincided in time with the modernization of the nation through active participation in national affairs by the increasingly broad popular masses. This, in turn, marked the final stage in the long process of replacing the old, historico-political conception of the Polish nation by a new, ethno-cultural conception. I have tried to show—and this is my most important conclusion—that all these processes were deeply interconnected and meaningfully related to each other. Economic modernization enabled the politicization of the masses which took the form of their "national awakening." This was a great historic achievement, putting an end to the long history where the national question was represented by only a minority, composed of the intelligentsia and the patriotic gentry. But the "nation of the people" could not have been a direct continuation of the "nation of the gentry." In a sense it was the beginning of something radically new—of the *modern* Polish nation, as a body embracing all strata of the Polish-speaking population.[1] This young modern nation, formed from below, under the influence of multiple ethnic conflicts in everyday life—at school, at the workplace, and at the marketplace—had to constitute itself as an overwhelmingly Roman Catholic ethno-linguistic entity, occupying the western part of the former Commonwealth of the gentry. Small wonder that it chose to stress its Western roots and defined its aspirations in terms of the Western civilizational option.

Among the political forces, the main credits for this development are due to both patriotic socialists, who acted among the industrial workers, and the National Democrats, who aroused national consciousness among the middle classes and the peasantry. For this reason it is justified to say that before 1914 the PPS (despite all its romantic and socialist illusions) and the *Endeks* (despite all the nasty features of their ideology), greatly contributed to the shaping of a modernized Polish nation. Whether this was an unambiguous improvement, or *only* an improvement, is an entirely different question.

In 1920 Polish workers and peasants, in defiance of communist internationalism, defended the newly restored "bourgeois Poland" against the invading Red Army. This was an enormous achievement of the "nationalization of the masses" brought about by modern ethno-linguistic nationalism. But the price for the growth of ethno-linguistic nationalism in the entire territory of the former Commonwealth proved to be terrible. The very beginning of the Polish independence coincided with the outbreak of a fratricidal struggle between Poles and Ukrainians in Eastern Galicia. The new People's Poland, created by Stalin and his Western allies at the end of World War II, did not emerge as an ethnically homogeneous national state: it became relatively homogeneous as a result of unprecedented resettlement operations which affected millions of people: Poles, Germans, Ukrainians, and Jews.

In contemporary Poland ethnic nationalism ceased to be needed as a factor nationalizing the masses and thus ensuring the cohesiveness of the nation. Because of this the older Polish tradition of non-ethnic, civic nationalism, in a modernized and thoroughly Westernized form, resumed its relevance, while ethnic nationalism degenerated into a xenophobic and increasingly anti-Western populism. It is significant, however, that civic patriotism in Poland avoids defining itself as a variety of nationalism. In the vocabulary of Polish politics the word "nation" (*naród*) retains its centrality but the word "nationalism" (*nacjonalizm*) is a pejorative term, reserved for the manifestations of a narrow-minded, intolerant ethnocentricity.

References

1.   Ivan L. Rudnytsky was right in maintaining that "the entire drift of historical development development in Central and Eastern Europe pointed toward a victory of ethnic self-determination over historical legitimism." (See Rudnytsky, "Polish-Ukrainian Relations: the Burden of History," in Peter J. Potichnyi, ed., *Poland and Ukraine: Past and Present* [Edmonton-Toronto, 1980], p. 24).

Text: Typeset at the Ukrainian Research Institute using Aldus PageMaker® 5.0, in 10.5 and 9.5 pt DCTimes, developed by Adrian Hewryk at the Ukrainian Research Institute. Printed by Thomson-Shore Printers, Inc. This booklet has been printed on long-lived acid-free paper.
Cover Design: R. De Lossa.
Inset: Detail from the Nova Totius Regni Poloniae, 1652 *of Guillaume Le Vasseur, Sieur de Beauplan, reproduced with the kind permission of Dr. Tomasz Niewodniczański of Bitburg, Germany.*
Map, page 8: Created with Adobe Illustrator® 3.0 by Adrian B. Hewryk and R. De Lossa.